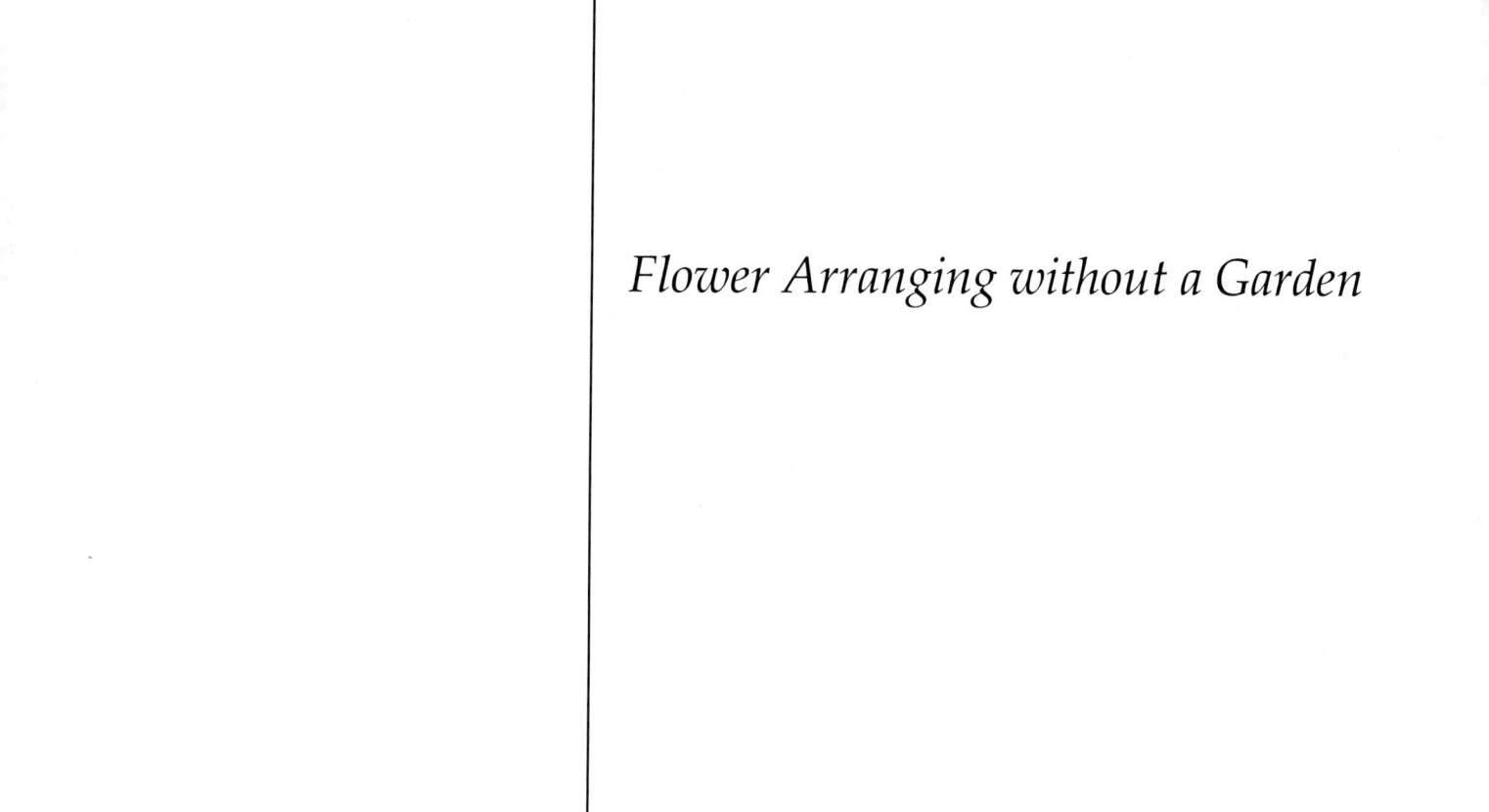

Flower Arranging without a Garden

Pauline Mann

Flower Arranging without a Garden

B.T. Batsford Ltd, London

To all flower arrangers who have no garden

Photographs by Derick Bonsall
Drawings by Wendy Goodwill

© Pauline Mann 1988
First published 1988

All rights reserved. No part of this publication may be reproduced, in any form or by any means, without permission from the Publisher

ISBN 0 7134 5457 1

Typeset by Tek-Art Ltd, Kent
and printed in Great Britain by
Anchor Brendon Ltd
Tiptree, Essex
for the publishers
B.T. Batsford Ltd
4 Fitzhardinge Street
London W1H 0AH

ACKNOWLEDGEMENTS

My gratitude to Wendy Goodwill NDD, DA (Manc) ATD, Lecturer in Art, York College of Arts and Technology, for doing the line drawings, and to Derick Bonsall ARPS, for taking the photographs.

Contents

Introduction — 9

CHAPTER 1 **Spring flowers** — 11

CHAPTER 2 **Summer flowers** — 24

CHAPTER 3 **Autumn flowers** — 36

CHAPTER 4 **Winter flowers and Christmas decorations** — 43

CHAPTER 5 **Pot-et-fleur**
Indoor plants combined with cut flowers — 66

CHAPTER 6 **Fruit, foliage and flowers**
Making a little go a long way — 81

CHAPTER 7 **Preserving plant material**
Methods of using glycerine, pressing, drying by hanging and with desiccants — 91

CHAPTER 8 **Aids to successful arranging**
Pinholders, wire netting, oasis, containers and bases. Lighting and displaying flower arrangements — 109

Appendix Wire measures — 125

Index — 126

Introduction

It is difficult for those with gardens (even the proverbial pocket handkerchief size) to imagine the frustration of trying to be a flower arranger without having any plot of land. In flower arranging today the leaves are as essential as the flowers; they are used for outline in the more traditional designs and also make a background against which the flowers show clearly. Often, enthusiastic would-be flower arrangers without a garden enrol for a class but soon find themselves depending on friends or the kindness and generosity of fellow students for foliage. Sometimes the tutor brings extra pieces, but this creates a precedent which can cause problems for others teaching the same subject. And it isn't only the foliage that is hard to come by: those who live in flats will also have to buy every flower. Many only buy a bunch as a treat and never have access to the mixture of blooms that the garden owner grows. In the end these once-hopeful arrangers feel inadequate and give up.

I have come across this frustration and disappointment many times and have always wanted to communicate my ideas for overcoming such problems. I especially love arrangements of one kind of flower, where I can really appreciate its characteristics and group it in a way that highlights these special qualities. This is why nearly all the designs in this book are made from a single bunch and are not mixed varieties: just sometimes I have been a little more extravagant and have bought two similar bunches or two different kinds of flower. Retailers often sell assorted bunches but they are usually the most incongruous mix of colours and sizes. This is an area of salesmanship which needs improvement – the idea is right but the execution wrong.

One essential piece of advice I would give to my readers is to abandon the urge to create mass arrangements. It is better instead to be unconventional and imaginative. Essentially I have concentrated on seasonal flowers which the arranger can obtain cheaply and easily. I have also included ways of using silk leaves, which are a useful standby if nothing else comes to hand. People living in flats in towns and cities don't see enough of the changes between spring, summer, autumn and winter, apart from alterations of light and temperature. All the exciting procession of the natural year provided by the hedgerows and fields is not on view, but it can be shown by flowers in the home. Some florists carry a marvellously varied stock, but there are many who have nothing other than chrysanthemums and carnations week in and week out. Seek out the market stalls, and try to find different flowers for each week of the year.

Over the last year I have visited the market weekly to see what has been on offer that is seasonal and a good buy; in so doing I have put myself into the position of the 'gardenless flower arranger', to whom this book is dedicated. I hope the text, drawings and photographs will give help and inspiration.

1
Spring flowers

When the Christmas decorations are finally put away on Twelfth Night I hate to return to the dried flowers that filled the gap between the end of the outdoor chrysanthemums and Christmas. It is exciting to look forward and to anticipate spring. Before Christmas, daffodils look out of place, but after 6 January they suddenly seem permissible and are in plentiful supply. The flowers are usually imported, though many will come from Cornwall; buy those in bud so that you can enjoy watching them open and make sure they have leaves, unless all you want is a block of colour.

DAFFODILS

All the daffodil or narcissus tribe originated around the Mediterranean and support the theory that land bridges previously existed that joined Morocco with Gibralta, Malta with Tunisia, and Sicily with Italy. Now the flowers are widely spread but interestingly there are none in the Americas in a wild state. Don't forget that the daffodil is the national emblem of Wales.

Preparation

There are certain things to look out for when choosing flowers that guarantee freshness, and I will point these out as I go along. Daffodils must look as if they are about to open, with a few slits in the sheaths showing yellow. If the flowers are too tightly in bud they may never come out properly. The bunches come in boxes packed close together and are commonly sold out of water; consequently the stem ends are quite dry and sealed over with callus and therefore unable to take up water.

When such a bunch is bought take it home and, holding the stems under water, cut off about 5 cm (2 in.), including all the white, pithy parts. Doing this under water prevents an air lock forming – it is also one of the easiest ways of curing one because the water will enter the freshly-cut stem ends with some pressure. Then place the daffodils in tepid water (this need not be deep), and leave them to drink for at least two hours before arranging them. If this simple practice is followed the buds will get the water necessary for their development and should last a week, providing conditions are not too hot. Try to put flowers in a cool place over night, and always top up the container or water the Oasis daily. Light spraying helps, too, in centrally-heated rooms.

Arranging

Daffodils are surprisingly versatile flowers – surprisingly, because they are by nature stiff and unyielding – but they lend themselves to many styles. They look good in a heavy modern glass container or even in an unusually-shaped glass jar. The

SPRING FLOWERS 13

1   Before Christmas daffodils look uncomfortably out of place, but in January they suddenly seem permissible.

2   Take the bunch home and, holding the stems under water, cut off about 5 cm (2 in.).

stems showing through the glass add to the balance of the design and are outlined with silver bubbles. Either vary the height of each flower, turning some to show their sides and backs with a three-dimensional effect, or use them to give a bold block of colour, similar to the anemones (colour plate 1). Use a twist of 2.5 cm or 5 cm (1 in. or 2 in.) wire netting, wedged near the top of the container to hold the stems. Spray or paint the wire silver to make it almost invisible.

Daffodils and wood

Daffodils and wood go well together, for the daffodil is an unsophisticated bloom that is matched by the earthiness of wood. Look out for a piece of wood with an interesting shape when in the country or on holiday. Wood can often be bought from a florist who stocks flower arranging aids, in which case it will already have been cleaned and may have been bleached. When you find a piece in the wild, clean it well and dig out any soft parts with a sharp knife. You can then lighten it by covering it with a solution of strong household bleach and water, or salt and water. It takes some time to change colour. After bleaching always rinse the wood thoroughly and dry it.

The surface may then be sanded, polished or stained in some way, but if the natural colour is attractive, leave it alone after making sure it will stand as you wish it to. To make it firm you

SPRING FLOWERS

may have to level it, screw it to a base or give it false legs. Cherish the piece of wood, for it will help a few flowers go a long way. When the wood is not screwed to a wood base, a base of some sort is necessary on which to stand it, along with a pinholder in a tin for the flowers. Thus the component parts of the design will be united by the base. A base is always needed when an accessory is used, or for more than one placement of flowers.

Five daffodils from a bunch of ten plus three ivy leaves from a pot plant or three silk leaves are all that you need with your wood to make a spring design (colour plate 2). The other five flowers and leaves from the bunch of ten can be made into a simple line arrangement, preferably in a vertical container of some kind, perhaps a homemade one (p. 117). Any strong-stemmed flowers as well as daffodils should be arranged in a slightly zig-zag line, each bloom showing a different aspect. The flower's own leaves can be cut and made into a fan shape at the back of the arrangement; this gives a more unusual effect.

Daffodils and water

Flowers are often associated with certain locations: for example foxgloves with woodland, heather with the moors and irises, reedmace and kingcups with water. Daffodils grow on the banks

3 *A flower commonly associated with woodland – the foxglove.*

of streams too – as Wordsworth noted – and look very pleasing and natural arranged in a shallow bowl. Place a pinholder on one side of the bowl, leaving space for the flowers to be reflected in the water. Use the leaves and cover the pinholder with stones. Any straight strong-stemmed flowers are successfully arranged this way, including gladioli, as the water surface balances their height. These water designs are best displayed on a low table, so that they can be viewed from above.

Daffodils in water-retaining foam

Daffodils, especially the early forced ones, don't readily go into water-retaining foam because their stems are too soft. Yet once they are fixed in the foam they last perfectly well. Either make holes in the foam with a 'prodder' or insert a drinking straw into the bottom 2.5–3.75 cm (1–1½ in.) of the stem, cutting off the straw flush with the stem end.

TULIPS

It is a pity not to buy tulips as they are not only varied and often flamboyant, particularly when wide open, but historically exciting too. Towards the latter half of the sixteenth and during the seventeenth centuries horticulture advanced rapidly, especially in Holland. The tulip, indigenous to Turkey, was introduced into Holland around 1562, and to England approximately 16 years later. By the year 1634 every Dutchman was growing tulips and was betting on how the bulbs would 'break' – that is, what colour patterns the blooms would have. The flecks and stripes on the petals were completely unpredictable and were caused by a virus infection, so the growers were able to place bets as to whether a flower would be a 'Byblomen' – white ground with rose and purple markings – or a 'Bizarre' – yellow ground with red markings. Fortunes were lost and made, and a single bulb changed hands for hundreds of pounds. Finally a law was passed to end the whole crazy business which had been dubbed 'Tulipomania'.

The Dutch/Flemish school of painters made good use of the tulip in their great compositions, depicting them, often with curved stems, arching across a multi-seasonal assortment of flowers that could not possibly have been out at the same time of the year. The pictures were really a collection of every flower Holland grew and were therefore pictorial floral catalogues.

Nowadays tulips are on sale in the shops and markets from January to May, although they can linger in the garden until June; they are, therefore, with us for half the year. There is nothing monotonous about them, however, for different species and cultivars appear each week. To begin with there are the single and double 'earlies', followed by vast numbers of other varieties. The latest in this procession are the most striking: the lily-flowered with their pointed petals; the Rembrandt, reminiscent of the Dutch/Flemish paintings, brownish and brightly striped; the fringed and parrot tulips, splashed with mixed colour; and the stately Darwins and large rounded peony-flowered kind – an enormous late assortment.

Preparation

It is best to look for tulips that are not too tightly in bud, especially early in the season. Choose a bunch where the buds are showing colour and look plump, not wizened. The foliage should be crisp and green and the stems strong. Tulips can be arranged in like manner to daffodils, but they are a far more sophisticated flower. It is a good plan to remove the lower leaves before the flowers are conditioned – keep them for later. Wrap the bunch in newspaper which will absorb water and envelope the flowers in moisture, as well as helping to keep the stems straight; tulips tend to 'grow' in water after they have been arranged and often need to be adjusted from time to time. Feeding them with half a teaspoonful of sugar or some proprietary brand of crystals in the conditioning water helps to strengthen the stems and encourage the buds to develop. Leave in water overnight if possible, even though the instructions on some tulip wrappings say two to three hours. Always cut the stems under water. Some people prick the stems with a pin just below the flower head; this is said to get rid of air locks, but I have never found it to make the slightest difference. Try turning the petals of well developed flowers back gently to open them wide (if you have never done this you will be surprised at the effect): the bloom becomes a large round shape showing all its markings and prominent anthers. When they are wide open float them on water in a shallow bowl and use it as a table arrangement. Accompanied by a suitable accessory or some dried wood and put onto a base, just two or three wide open flowers are striking.

BLOSSOM

I am never sure if it is blossom or the early daffodils which are the quintessence of spring. Perhaps the season could be divided into two, with daffodils symbolizing early spring and blossom heralding late spring turning to summer. Finding blossom to buy is not easy, but at the beginning of February there should be branches of forced forsythia, with brilliant yellow flowers on the leafless stems, available in florists' shops. Almond blossom, forced lilac and *Prunus triloba* also appear; the latter with stiff stems, but very delicate pink blossom.

If blossom is difficult or expensive to come by it is quite easy

SPRING FLOWERS

to make a silk blossom branch. All you need is a well-shaped bare branch of a size suitable for the home; hawthorn is interesting because of its rugged growth, and it is not difficult to find. Then buy a single spray of small silk flowers, either pink or white. It is a very simple operation to glue the little flowers to the natural branch. Look at a picture of plum, apple or pear blossom so that the distribution of the flowers is realistic. A branch such as this can stay in position for a while with different small flowers at its base and a few silk leaves added to them to cover the pinholder. It makes an attractive 'landscape' style arrangement.

THE COMMON PRIMROSE (Primula vulgaris)

Very frequently there are bunches of the wild primroses on sale; the pale yellow flowers wreathed with their knobbly leaves; the pinkish stems bound with soft wool. Nothing smells quite so fresh and clean or appears as innocent as primroses. The wool or rubber band binding the stems should be loosened before you cut a small amount off the stems and put them in a little container of water. They are perfection by themselves. *Keep them cool* and lightly sprayed.

4   Very frequently bunches of wild primroses are on sale.

Primroses have several names used in different parts of the country: 'Easter Rose', 'Darling of April', 'Lent Rose' and 'Golden Stars' are some of them, and they are so pretty. Primroses were the favourite flowers of Queen Victoria's Prime Minister, Disraeli. The Queen is reported to have sent a wreath of them to his funeral.

Treat any of the small spring flowers in the same way: grape hyacinths, chionodoxa, scillas and violets all need to be clustered together or their impact is lost. Violets need even more moisture then primroses, so spray them often.

POLYANTHUS

The word polyanthus means 'many-flowered', and this describes this member of the *Primulaceae* family beautifully. The pots of brightly coloured flowers begin to arrive before Christmas and increase in number during the first months of the year. Their popularity has escalated considerably over the last decade, probably because it is almost impossible to resist their brilliant hues, clear and jewel-like. The Pacific strain includes the colours blue, red, yellow, orange, pink and white.

Polyanthus make the perfect addition to a pot-et-fleur (p. 66). To do this sink a whole pot into the growing compost or simply place it amongst the other pots, depending on which method has been employed for the making. When the polyanthus plant is to go at the foot of the blossom branch, first water it before inverting the pot and letting the plant fall into your hand. Remove some of the bottom soil carefully before wrapping the roots and remaining soil in a polythene bag to prevent it from drying out. This bundle can be concealed by the leaves or moss at the base of the branch, but don't forget to open the bag and water the plant. If a polyanthus with plenty of buds has been chosen, it should continue flowering for many weeks.

A rather more extravagant way of enjoying polyanthus is to buy several pots and group them in a basket. Line the basket with polythene or something that will hold water and choose a deep enough basket to hide the plastic pots.

PUSSY WILLOW

Pussy willow is sold in bundles in shops and markets quite early in the year. It is a good buy, as it harmonizes with daffodils and tulips, and you can also treat it with glycerine to preserve it. The flower arranger without a garden, therefore, has a ready source of outline material for arrangements throughout the year with pussy willow. On the subject of glycerine – it can be used for leaves, seedheads and bracts (these are flower-like leaves) but not flowers. Instructions are on page 93. It is useful to have a

SPRING FLOWERS

bottle of glycerine at hand for use when the right pieces of foliage unexpectedly come to hand, such as the odd fatshedera leaf or fern frond from indoor plants, or the surprise 'find' from an expedition into the country.

There are many species of willow, not all native to Britain. Some are cut back regularly to make small bushes that will provide colourful shoots in winter. A willow with red stems is *Salix 'Chermesina'*, the coral bark willow, and it is this species which is available in early spring. Except on an occasional weeping willow all have either male or female flowers on separate trees. The bunches sold for flower arranging are male, covered eventually with rich golden pollen.

Pussy willow branches have become associated with Palm Sunday and have been adopted as symbols of Christ's ride into Jerusalem on the back of a donkey. In winter all willows look very alert with their shiny bark. The weeping willow is one of the first trees to put out leaves in the early spring. They are a wonderfully graceful sight when their new, lime-green, pendulous branches move in the wind.

5 *Pussy willow is sold in bundles quite early in the year.*

2
Summer flowers

PERENNIALS

Flowers know when they should bloom even if our weather doesn't encourage them! From the beginning of spring until mid-summer nature is in a hurry, eager to produce flowers that will set seed and so complete the reproduction cycle once more. The perennials are the best example of this zeal, for no sooner have the late frosts finished than they grow very quickly. A perennial is a plant that dies down during the winter but reappears in spring year after year: pyrethrums, delphiniums, lupins, peonies, scabious, pinks and campanulas are amongst the first summer perennials to bloom. The predominating colours of the summer garden before August are blue, white and pink. Later the garden produces many yellow flowers: rudbeckia, heleniums, gaillardias and helianthus are the commonest. The dahlia, one of the most successfully commercialized of flowers, is a later summer one, so are the gladioli. Most of these should be on sale both in shops and on market stalls.

ANNUALS

Some of the most attractive flowers to look out for are the annuals; these have only one season's life span – they take one growing season to complete the life cycle from seed to seed. There are two categories of annual: the hardy, which can safely

6

7

8

6 A perennial is a plant that dies down during the winter but reappears in spring year after year; the delphinium is an example.

7 Campanulas are some of the first perennials to bloom.

8 The perennial rudbeckias come later in the summer.

be planted outside in March or April; and the half-hardy, which needs protection from frost and should not be planted outside until all danger of it has gone. Amongst these two sorts of annual is to be found a wide variety of shapes and colours, and although they are not notably long lasting they give tremendous pleasure to the flower arranger.

SELECTING FRESH FLOWERS

Some advice on choosing summer and early autumn flowers will be useful. I have already given some advice on what to look for when purchasing spring flowers, so at the end of this chapter tips are included on detecting whether a flower is fresh, along with the ways in which tired blooms may be revitalized.

The origin and propagation of plants is obscure and amazing. But birds and animals have played their part in the process and men have carried roots, cuttings and seeds from one place to another so that over the centuries species of flora have been distributed all over the world. It is fascinating to find out a plant's place of origin because this will reveal the conditions necessary for its welfare; but it also shows how very adaptable many shrubs and trees are, whilst others cannot cope with the wrong soil, wrong amount of humidity and wrong temperature.

Yet strains and varieties are always being created: thousands have been produced by cross-fertilization processes over the centuries. Nature has done her share of this as well as man so there are always new varieties, colours, petal shapes, as well as attempts to make plants resistant to disease. Because of this the botanical scene constantly changes; nevertheless there is a background of myths and legends attached to the oldest flowers that have persisted throughout the centuries.

ROSES

For those without a garden the only choice of rose will be a variety from the florist. However beautiful these are, they haven't the generosity or perfume of their garden-grown relatives. Country stalls in markets usually have bunches of roses for sale during the summer and these are worth finding.

The rose is the favourite flower of so many people that even the least knowledgeable on floral matters will recognize it. It has an intriguing history for its fossils have been found in Colorado and Oregon, dating back 30 million years. Walter De la Mare encapsulated the general sentiment in his poem 'All that's Past', with the words:

Oh, no man knows
Through what wild centuries
Roves back the rose.

9 *The rose: a flower with an intriguing history.*

CORNFLOWERS

The botanical name for the cornflower is *Centaurea cyanus* because legend has it that the flower healed a wound in the foot of Chiron, one of the centaurs of Ancient Greece. It was once very common in the wild and plentiful in Great Britain in the late glacial period, later invading corn fields. Now with the use of selective weed killers it is seldom seen in the fields. Introduced into gardens and much loved by the Tudors, today its popularity has revived. It dries extremely well in a desiccant.

DIANTHUS (Carnations and Pinks)

The name comes from the Greek – *dios*, a god or divine, and *anthos*, a flower. It is one of the oldest known and most sweetly scented of garden flowers, and has had much written about it. In the first century AD Pliny recorded that the clove carnation was discovered in Spain in the days of Augustus Caesar, and that the Spaniards used it to add spice to their drinks; a practice that was followed by other people including the English. The strongly scented dianthus was called 'Sops-in-wine' and the name held throughout Tudor times. When Gerard and Parkinson wrote their herbals in the late fifteenth and early sixteenth centuries the dianthus had already been in this country for a long time, possibly imported amongst the building stones from France by the Normans at the time of the Conquest. The two herbalists made a distinction between the larger carnation and the gillyflower – the name given by the Tudors to all the clove-scented flowers: stocks, wallflowers, sweet williams and dianthus.

By the middle of the eighteenth century carnations – the large ones that we know by that name today – had become one of the florists' flowers; they still are. The others at that time were the auricula, polyanthus, hyacinth, tulip, anemone and ranunculus. Interestingly, the name 'pink' is nothing to do with the colour but is possibly a reference to the flower's small *twink*ling eye.

Many sitters for portraits held a pink in their hand or had one pinned to their person. There is a well known painting of Anne of Cleves by Holbein in which Anne holds a carnation. The significance of this was that the dianthus or carnation symbolized betrothal, and the picture is reputed to be the one sent to Henry VIII before his first meeting with his bride-to-be. The flower also stands for both divine and earthly love.

CAMPANULA

The campanula belongs to a genus of over 250 species, which includes hardy annuals, half-hardy annuals, biennials (flowers that take two years to complete their cycle) and perennials. The campanula arranged in the tea-pot (colour plate 8) is a perennial called *Campanula persicifolia* 'Planiflora Alba'. Campanula come into bloom about the beginning of July in the north of England but probably earlier in the south. Understandably they are known as 'bell flowers', and the biennial species, *Campanula media*, is the Canterbury bell. In one form this produces bell-like flowers surrounded by a calyx of the same colour – the 'cup-and-saucer' variety. Campanula are blue or white, sometimes the blue is almost purple or mauve; only in the Canterbury bell is there a pink and apricot form. There is an extremely pretty pot variety – *Campanula isophylla* – which looks beautiful in a pot-et-fleur, being one of the cascading kind.

DELPHINIUMS AND LARKSPUR

The delphiniums grown as perennials in our gardens belong to the species *Delphinium elatum*, which has been with us since the seventeenth century. The larkspur is *Delphinium consolida*, a common species found growing in our country as far back as 1572. Its flowers, when distilled, were said to improve the sight and to help in the healing of wounds. Today's branching, free-flowering annuals are descendants of this plant. As a cut flower it is surprisingly long lasting and it also dries successfully. Although the range of blue is not as extensive as in the perennial it has several pink forms of bright fresh colours. When the stems of flowers are dry, spray them with hair lacquer to stop the petals from dropping.

GLADIOLI

The name gladioli comes from the Latin *gladiolus*, meaning 'a little sword', and the flowers are sometimes called 'sword lilies'. The sword-like part of the plant is the leaf. They grow from corms and are half-hardy. Gladioli are a very worthwhile buy for people without gardens because they last quite a long time if they are bought in bud – their leaves are also a bonus for the flower arranger. Like the carnation, rose, freesia, gerbera and several other flowers, the gladiolus numbers amongst those that are available all year round. Its popularity is phenomenal and there is tremendous variety with the vast number of cultivars that have appeared over the years. Sadly, however, it has no scent.

Many species are indigenous to Europe, Asia Minor and South Africa, but Britain has a native species, *Gladiolus illyricus*, which is found very rarely in the New Forest and the Isle of Wight. Gerard, the herbalist, grew the two European species, *Gladiolus communis* and *Gladiolus segetum*, in 1597, but in the last century when hybridization began, the choice became far more extensive. There are now some miniature primulinus and butterfly hybrids with exquisitely marked throats. The colour range is considerable, the only missing hue being that of a true blue.

Gladioli are tall, heavy flowers and need strong and weighty mechanics (see p. 117). They look best arranged as they grow, vertically, and are ideal for the pot-et-fleur – three, or at the most five, being enough for this. Cut the stems so that they step down in height. A 7.5 cm (3 in.) pinholder firmly fixed in its tin or a well pinholder are best for putting in the pot-et-fleur. Any narrow vertical container suits these flowers. Even a tall milk bottle with a screw of wire netting wedged in the top will hold two or three stems in the correct position; more than three may prove to be too heavy for the bottle. It can be disguised with a pop-over cover.

Annuals to look out for during the summer
Amaranthus caudatus (love-lies-bleeding – red variety)
Amaranthus viridis (love-lies-bleeding – green variety)
antirrhinum (snapdragon)
aster
Centaurea cyanus (cornflower)
cosmos
larkspur
Molucella laevis (bells of Ireland)
nicotiana (tobacco flowers)

stocks
sweet peas
trollius
zinnia

To be dried
achillea
anaphalis (pearl everlasting)
echinops (globe thistle)
eryngium (sea holly)
Helichrysum bracteatum (straw flower)
helipterum
Physalis franchetti (Chinese lanterns)
Statice dumosum
Statice sinuatum
Statice suworowii

CHOOSING FRESH FLOWERS

Look at the flower stems. Discoloured and/or smelly stems with or without decomposing leaves tell you that the flowers have been in water a very long time.

Flagging foliage may indicate that the flowers have been out of water too long *or* that they have just been unpacked and are fresh but in need of a drink, so examine them for other signs of age.

When buying flowers that grow in spikes – delphiniums,

larkspur and gladioli, for example – select those that have the bottom blooms just opening and the top blooms still in bud.

Double flowers, such as carnations, need to have tightly curled centres. If the centre is loose and showing stamens it is fully open and past its best. Single flowers, including lilies, should have pale pollen adhering tightly to the anthers. Dark and loose pollen grains denote an ageing flower.

Flower petals should feel crisp and must not be crepey or discoloured.

GETTING THE BEST FROM THE BUNCH

In order to persuade every bud to open in a bunch take off some of the leaves; this stops flowers and foliage competing for moisture. Cut off dead flowers to encourage the buds to open. A very small amount of sugar – a quarter of a teaspoonful to a pint of water – nourishes cut flowers.

A fresh flower can wilt, but all flowers should live out their life span if treated properly. If a flower wilts before its time it is usually caused by an air lock in the stem which is preventing it from taking up water. This is why you should cut stems afresh before conditioning.

Below are some first aid treatments.
- Re-cut the stem under water, removing about 5 cm (2 in.). Put

into deep tepid water at once.
- Re-cut the stem as above, then allow the entire flower to float on water for two hours.
- Defoliate and re-cut as above and then completely submerge the flower for a short time.
- Re-cut and defoliate, then protect the flower head with tissue paper or a soft cloth before putting the stem into 2.5 cm (1 in.) of boiling water. Leave the flower in the water until it cools, then fill up with tepid water and leave for a short time before arranging. This last method never fails to revive a flagging rose.

3
Autumn flowers

It is strange that although autumn foreshadows the death of the year, it also carries with it a feeling of renewal. So many activities are started at this season; children embark on a new school or a new school year; the university year begins; it is the time for enrolment for evening classes of all possible kinds, including flower arranging; musical societies commence their winter programme; and clubs meet again after the refreshing summer break. In the garden it is time for replanning the beds and borders, for replacing shrubs, for receiving the boxes of bulbs ordered from seductive glossy catalogues, which in a few weeks give a taste of spring as the overwhelming scent of hyacinths floods the room.

The autumn colours are mature, the sunshine a rich deep yellow. The mornings are hazy and the dew so thick that the grass barely has time to dry out before it is evening again. The haste that nature appeared to be in when summer came has disappeared; the autumn lingers as lazily as the dying light after a brilliant October day.

It is the season for berries and cones and for all kinds of fruit, both edible and inedible. It is true chrysanthemum time, and there will be masses of the outdoor kinds in shops and markets. It is also time to arrange the dried flowers bought in July – and how pleased you will be that you wired the helichrysums before drying them. Perhaps an attempt could be made to make a pressed picture and begin hoarding for Christmas decorations. It seems that, after all, autumn is full of promise, not in any way an end, but a beginning.

DAHLIAS

Dahlias predict summer's almost imperceptible mergence with autumn. The blooms make the market stalls glow from the end of July until the frosts finally cut them down; this sometimes happens quite early in September, whilst in gentler years they can continue in flower until the end of October. The colours are rich and strong and they make the chrysanthemums appear very muted. Dahlias are half-hardy, tuberous-rooted perennials; the tubers have to be dug up for the winter, dried, and stored in a frost-free place. It takes only one sharp frost to blacken the dahlias and finish them for the year.

With a flower as popular and ubiquitous as the dahlia, it is difficult to realize that it is a comparative newcomer to these islands. These flowers, with their brilliant barbaric hues, are natives of Mexico and were not introduced to Europe until the latter part of the eighteenth century. Their name derives from the Swedish botanist, Dr Dahl, who was involved in the

10 *Dahlias make the markets glow with colour from late July until the frost begins.*

attempts to acclimatize the plant in the Old World. Apparently, Dr Dahl and a Frenchman, a Monsieur Thouin, thought they were dealing with another tuberous-rooted vegetable similar to the potato, and they gave dahlia tubers to men and cattle to eat: neither found them the least bit palatable. It was in France that improvements were achieved on the dahlia, and the species *Dahlia pinnata* is said to have been planted by the Empress Josephine in her garden at Malmaison. After peace was made with France in 1814 dahlias were imported into Britain and during the next 20 years they became a most fashionable flower. Nurserymen have been experimenting with them ever since and there are now many forms: single, anemone flowered, ball, peony-flowered, pompom, cactus-flowered and others, some of giant proportions. What a pity such a commercially-successful flower has no scent.

CHRYSANTHEMUMS

Chrysanthemums must be the most commercially rewarding flowers grown in this country. Their natural season is the autumn, but as some varieties are not hardy these have always been protected by glass to procure blooms for winter decoration. But nowadays during the whole year many millions of little plants are brought into flower by doses of imposed darkness and controlled artificial light and sold in their pots under the rather insulting label of 'Mums'. Also, throughout the year, stems of spray chrysanthemums are available at any time and seem to be a part of most flower arrangements. This over-use is not the fault of the flower but comes from its priceless virtue of being very long lasting.

Chrysanthemum parthenium, our feverfew, recommended for migraine and arthritis sufferers, is generally believed to be native to this country. The real chrysanthemum has not been here all that long although Confucius is said to have mentioned it in 500 BC. It did not reach us until the end of the eighteenth century. It did, however, spread to Japan where it became the national flower as early as AD 400. Once this flower reached the West growers set about improving it and have gone on doing so ever since, for there are now hundreds of cultivars.

The perfection of the large tea-plate sized blooms is admirable, reflecting the dedicated workmanship that goes into their production. To me the 'incurved' are the least desirable for they look so solid, whilst some of the reflexed exhibition varieties are attractively tousle-headed. The rayonnante type, with thread-like petals, the anemone and single-flowered have become most popular with flower arrangers, but none are more sought after than the always-available, many-coloured sprays. Because they are tenacious of life they are practical for use in swags, garlands, topiary trees and cones. The white spray 'Bonny Jean' is especially liked, with its wide-eyed innocent daisy blossoms. Even one spray – or stem – will supply enough flowers for a small arrangement. A stem should be chosen for the individual length of the stem of each flower, and must be carefully cut so that the length is preserved. Don't buy when the flowers are tightly clustered together on very short stems.

Chrysanthemums mix well with fruit in an arrangement, and the great winter 'mop heads' go nicely in a pot-et-fleur.

NERINES

It is strange and surprising how a flower that has been considered a luxury for years suddenly becomes commonplace. This has happened to several lilies, especially the orange 'Enchantment' and the yellow 'Destiny', now both available the whole year round. These may still cost quite a lot at the best florists, but can be bought at market stalls and street barrows for very small sums indeed. The nerine does not yet fall into this category but during the last five years or so has become much easier to find and is not especially expensive to buy. Yet in previous years they were hardly known, except to the enthusiastic gardener, and were considered rare and exotic.

The nerine's native habitat was thought to be Japan, and the

Nerine sarniensis – the 'Guernsey lily' – is so called because the plant was apparently included in the Japanese cargo of a Dutch or English ship that was wrecked on Guernsey. This tale was told in a book published in 1680, but it appears that nerines were mentioned by John Evelyn earlier than this in his *Kalendarium Hortensis* in 1664. The true date of the flower's introduction to this country will never be known, but it has been found that the nerine is also indigenous to South Africa where there are about 30 known species. Francis Masson, a plant collector at Kew, recorded the *Nerine sarniensis* growing wild about the Cape during his expedition in 1772.

The commercialized variety of nerine is *Nerine bowdenii*. This is one of the hardier South African species which can be grown outside in this country if protected by a south-facing wall or some sheltered place where the bulbs will be baked by the summer sun. This species was collected by Mr Athelstan Bowden who sent some bulbs home to his mother in Devon at the end of the last century. She eventually presented some to Kew. Species other than bowdenii need cool greenhouse protection. The *Nerine bowdenii* is a shocking pink; the petals are slightly crinkled and possess an iridescence which is quite unusual. They are members of the *Amaryllis* family and have a characteristic sappy smell. Like most lilies they are long lasting.

SCHIZOSTYLIS (Kaffir Lily)

The name Kaffir lily explains the origin of these flowers for they are another of South Africa's contributions to the more unusual blooms that are now enjoyed in Britain. Sold in bunches during the late autumn they look rather insignificant at first glance, but they are long lasting, uncommon and inexpensive. In appearance the Kaffir lily resembles a miniature gladiolus; not surprisingly they belong to the same family. To judge by the number on sale they must grow quite prolifically, and they do not seem to have been 'improved' as yet. The colours are restricted to a pale and darker pink. They are, however, well worth looking out for.

11   *In appearance the schizostylus or Kaffir lily resembles a miniature gladiolus. They are on sale during the late autumn.*

4
Winter flowers and Christmas decorations

When does winter begin? I like to think winter is confined to the months of November and December and that spring begins on Boxing Day; after all, the days start to lengthen after 21 December, and once the climax of Christmas is over it is natural to look forwards. Unfortunately, winter threatens from the moment the first frost flattens the dahlias and the outdoor chrysanthemums are battered and soggy. The well-stocked florist's window belies the desolation outside, with its plenteous supplies of roses, carnations, freesias, gerberas, anemones, varied lilies and, of course, chrysanthemums, whose season it truly is from September until Christmas. None of the florist's display has had to battle with icy winds, relentless rain, the threat of snow and inevitable frost. The shop window flowers have led controlled and protected lives, justifying their high prices. In the dark world far removed from the warm greenhouses and lighted shop windows, the shrubs and trees are going about their business preparing to put out new leaves in the coming spring. As early as January – and sometimes sooner if the season is mild – they carry swollen buds on their branches that glisten in the sunlight or in the car's headlamps at night.

Any winter garden has interest, but the town or city dweller often fails to appreciate this. Living plants in a pot-et-fleur will sustain the feeling of life until it is time for the Christmas decorations; and what better flowers could there be for the pot-et-fleur than chrysanthemums? During the long evenings Christmas decorations can be made which, when the time comes, will give brightness and sparkle to the darkest part of the year. Then, one day, when you look into a flower shop there will be snowdrops, confirming that the year's cycle has begun again.

SNOWDROPS

The time when snowdrops come into flower in the garden, or appear in the shops tied with ivy leaves, varies greatly according to the region. In Cornwall and western coastal regions with their softer climates, flowers appear in January, but further north and east it will be February or March before they whiten the ground.

The *Galanthus nivalis* – or snowdrop – may not be native to Britain. It is said to have been brought from Italy by monks during the fifteenth century, whilst a larger kind, *Galanthus plicatus*, came from the Crimea. No flower is more typical of late winter than these. In the days when life was dictated by the church calendar, Christmas could go on until Candlemas, a festival that falls on 2 February. It isn't hard to see that, apart from having to look after stock, the long haul between Christmas and Candlemas was not a period of intensive work for farmers,

12   *No flower is more typical of late winter than the snowdrop.*

for there was no machinery, no electricity and precious little transport. Prolonging the Christmas jollifications would add a grain of spice to the long, dark days. Candlemas day was a feast in honour of the purification of the Virgin Mary and Christ's presentation in the temple. The snowdrop was the flower of the feast in this country. It had many other names: 'Fair maid of February', 'Candlemas bells', 'Purification flower', 'White lady' and 'Snowflower', and another, perhaps the most apt, 'Mary's tapers'.

The delicious small blossoms are edged with green on the short inner petals; the green is not easy to see unless you look into the flower rather than down upon it. It is amazing that anything that has such a fragile air should be so tough, standing up to all sorts of winter weather and quite unabashed by snow. Like all small flowers they are best bunched together when picked, tied with soft wool or held in a rubber band – but loosely, so that the stems are not bruised. They fit beautifully into a landscape design under the silk blossom branch, or if several bunches are purchased they can be massed in four small glasses. If there are no ivy leaves accompanying the snowdrops, take a few from an indoor plant because green is essential to bring out the startling whiteness to the full. Keep them as cool as possible; if they are taken out of a heated room over night they may last a week.

ANEMONES

The richly-coloured anemones in the shops and markets are usually *Anemone 'De Caen'* or *A. 'St Brigid'*, and they are in season all year round. The bunches are always of mixed colours and include red, deep purple-blue, shades of cyclamen, mauve and white: mostly hot, vivid colours from the warm side of the spectrum. No foliage comes with the flowers other than their decorative green calyxes, which give them character. Anemones belong to a large group that contains about 150 species, many of which are indigenous to Mediterranean areas. Some scholars think that the 'lilies of the field', referred to by Christ in the Sermon on the Mount, were wild anemones which grow abundantly in Palestine. Earlier than this, *Anemone coronaria* – from which species *A. 'De Caen'* and *A. 'St Brigid'* are descended – were used in garlands in ancient Greece and Rome. Anemones are also called 'wind flowers', this pretty name deriving from the notion that they do not open by themselves but only when the wind blows.

Anemones need careful selection in the shops and very thorough conditioning. Like most fleshy-stemmed flowers, they

13 Anemones are sold in bunches of mixed colours that include red, deep purple-blue, shades of cyclamen, mauve and white.

WINTER FLOWERS AND CHRISTMAS DECORATIONS

don't like being in water-retaining foam and last their best when their stems are in deep water. When choosing them – and do try to buy a couple of bunches at a time – make certain the buds are plump and showing colour. Their beauty lies in their colour and they need to be massed so that the brilliant hues are seen close together. Cut off 2.5 cm (1 in.) of stem under water and then put them into tepid water up to their necks. The flowers will respond by opening slowly and revealing their circle of dark stamens against the 'stained glass' colours of the petals. A deep blue or black pot shows off their richness. Crumpled wire will support the stems perfectly. If a flower wilts or refuses to open properly try the hot water treatment (p. 35), but only immerse the very end of the stem.

FREESIAS

Freesias are natives of South Africa, named after an Austrian botanist, Dr Freece. They are not hardy. These sweetly scented delicate flowers tend to vanish in mixed arrangements and are best enjoyed in a vase by themselves. Although they can be had all the year round, their most plentiful season is from January until April; it is then that the bunches of separate colours are

14   *Freesias are sweetly scented delicate flowers.*

easiest to come by. Try to find a narrow-necked bottle similar to those used many years ago as part of an old-fashioned cruet – one that held vinegar. Failing this any small-necked bottle of approximately 15 cm (6 in.) high will do. If it isn't an attractive bottle give it a pop-on cover. As the little trumpets wilt, remove them carefully to encourage the buds to open. Freesias are always a popular choice for wedding bouquets and head-dresses because of their soft colouring, scent, shape and size.

HELLEBORES

The hellebore, or Christmas rose, must have more legends attached to it than almost any other flower. The prefix 'Christmas' goes back to Christian beginnings, but the flower was valued by the ancient Greeks for its medicinal properties. It was considered to be a cure for insanity, and because of this virtue was probably brought to Britain by the Romans.

The Christmas rose, *Helleborus niger*, is only one of several species. Even without its important medicinal powers, the *Helleborus niger* is a notable plant, for it is one of the first flowers to uncoil from the earth and brave the rigours of December and January. The species *niger* is the whitest of the genus; the word 'niger' refers to the blackness of the root. The petals are actually tiny tubular sepals in a ring round the anthers.

15   *This is one of the many species of hellebore,* Helleborus orientalis. *The plastic hellebores in colour plate 12 are copies of* Helleborus niger – *the Christmas rose.*

At Christmas time the *Helleborus niger* is hard to condition; all sorts of exotic methods are bandied about, including using gin instead of water. Arranging in water and never in Oasis is one of the safest ways, but allow the flowers to float for a couple of hours, having first broken the outer skin of the stem along its entire length with a pin. Later, when the seed-cases swell, these flowers will last for weeks, as will all the other species.

Unfortunately, fresh hellebores are not often found for sale, but plastic and silk or polyester ones abound during the run up to Christmas. The silk and polyester ones are pretty and dainty, but the plastic sort are the most realistic because the real flowers have rather thick and waxy sepals, which plastic best emulates. These are cheap to buy and their stems can be lengthened with wire to give some variety in height.

CHRISTMAS

Some kind of fever affects flower arrangers during the months of November and December. They attend classes for making decorations; buy Christmas editions of magazines containing instructions for the same; scour the shops; and beleaguer flower club stalls for gold and silver plastic leaves smothered with glitter. During the festive season sparkling crinkle-foil paper is made into strange flower shapes and simple crepe paper

WINTER FLOWERS AND CHRISTMAS DECORATIONS

carnations are plentiful. There are ribbon flowers, felt flowers and flowers made from old tights, first bleached and then dyed, before being stretched over petal-shaped frames of wire. Cones are sprayed gold or silver or whitened with artificial snow.

There are many people who prefer their Christmas decorations to be of traditional fresh holly, ivy and other evergreens; they are often country dwellers for whom the hedgerows will yield foliage if their gardens cannot. For those who have no trees to hand, the market stalls cater well, providing boughs of holly and bunches of mistletoe. When living plant material is preferred and is used for an arrangement it will stay fresh for the twelve days of Christmas if you treat it properly and put it into water or some kind of moisture-retaining material (soaked Oasis, wet sand or moss). When fresh foliage is mixed with artificial it is best to tape the wire stems so that they do not rust. Wire stems have a habit of swinging around in either wet or dry Oasis and tape will help to prevent this. If the artificial material is very heavy the addition of a tripod foot will hold it in place. When things to be stored have been in water, do dry them properly before putting them away or they will go mouldy.

Today the artificial has become acceptable to nearly everyone; even the die-hards buy a plastic tree which will not shed its needles. A collection of plastic holly, ivy, mistletoe, Christmas

16   *If the artificial plant material is very heavy the addition of a tripod foot will stop it from swinging around in the Oasis.*

roses, poinsettias and fruits can be built up year by year so that different styles and colour schemes are possible. There is great scope for creativity at Christmas time, and the use of the artificial does permit decorations to be made well in advance so that the last minute rush is avoided.

Basically there are three categories of Christmas decoration, depending on the mechanics.

- The straightforward arrangement which employs ordinary mechanics: pinholder, Oasis (wet or dry) and moss.
- Decorations using plaster to make a semi-permanent arrangement that can be stored away for another year, including: topiary trees of all sizes, scenes – especially those for children – and even table arrangements.
- The decorations that depend on a wire frame, wire netting or upon being wired together in some way. These are the door wreaths, swags and garlands, the latter being rope-like decorations to drape above a fireplace or surround a door case.

Making a topiary tree

The Romans are thought to have brought the art of topiary to Britain. The word topiary comes from the Latin *topiarius*, meaning ornamental gardening. Yew, box and other slow-growing evergreens have been cut into decorative shapes for hundreds of years. Elizabethan and Jacobean gardeners especially loved topiary, and with the arrival of William and Mary from Holland in 1689 this fashion reached its peak and has never again attained such popularity.

Flower arrangers have appropriated the term 'topiary' for the various decorated versions of round or triangular shaped trees made in all sizes in pots. They can be of artificial or fresh material but they all appear clipped in outline, which justifies the use of the word 'topiary'. The arrival of the various water-retaining foams, dry foams and polystyrene shapes means that the mechanics for the trees are simple. (Those made from fresh flowers and foliage are most acceptable for weddings or other special events. They will need wet Oasis covered with cling film and enclosed in wire to give the Oasis extra strength. Always cut the stems of the plant material on the slant so that there is a point to penetrate the foam.) The Christmas or dried flower versions are made on the polystyrene shapes and usually need the material to be given wire stems. These stems go into the polystyrene very easily.

Covering a pot with fabric
- Measure the height of the pot and the circumference of its top and bottom.
- Cut a template to these measurements. Place the template on the cross of the fabric and cut around it.

- Take care to use a glue that will not mark the fabric. Many well known adhesives are made especially for using with cloth – 'Marvin' is excellent.
- When the pot is covered, braid may be added to the top and bottom as a finishing touch.

Fixing the 'trunk'

For small pots use a pot plant cane. Be sure it is long enough – the cane can always be shortened but never lengthened. A rough guide for the height of the tree is that its top should never reach *LESS* than one and a half times the height of the pot used. Sometimes the tree needs to be taller than this: if it is too close to the pot it will appear heavy and dumpy. If too much 'trunk' shows between the pot and the tree it seems divorced from its container. It is all a matter of good proportion, and the eye can be trained to appreciate this.

For pots with larger diameters of 10 cm (4 in.) upwards to 30 cm (12 in.), dowelling rod of a suitable calibre should be substituted for the cane 'trunk'. If the pot is over 30 cm (12 in.), a broom handle will be needed. Before either the broom handle or dowelling rod are set in concrete, drill small holes through them, one near to the top and the other at the place where the lower end of the Oasis (wet or dry) will come (see fig. 17, p. 56). The holes allow reel wire to be passed through them and fastened to the wire netting covering the Oasis foam. Or make the holes large enough to take a peg of some kind; either reel wire or a peg will prevent the foam from sliding down the rod.

To fix the rods
— Fill one third to one half of the pot with sand or small pebbles and then top up with concrete to 2.5 cm (1 in.) from the rim of the pot. Concrete is the cheapest thing to use for large containers, but Polyfilla (cellulose filler) can be more convenient for smaller ones.
— Put the rod or broom handle into the concrete, taking care that it is dead centre and remains so as the Polyfilla hardens.
— When the Polyfilla has dried, the surface and the rod should be painted or sprayed: perhaps gold for Christmas, but brown or green if the tree base is to be used throughout the year.

Mechanics
Once you have fixed the tree trunk the mechanics must be added. The illustration on page 56. fig. 18, shows how to fasten on the soaked Oasis. If the tree is to be decorated with artificial material, a polystyrene ball or cone (instead of Oasis) will need to be put on to the rod. The polystyrene shapes should be sprayed before they are decorated so that the background blends in unobtrusively with whatever artificial plant material is used. Metallic sprays melt polystyrene if used too lavishly, so spray

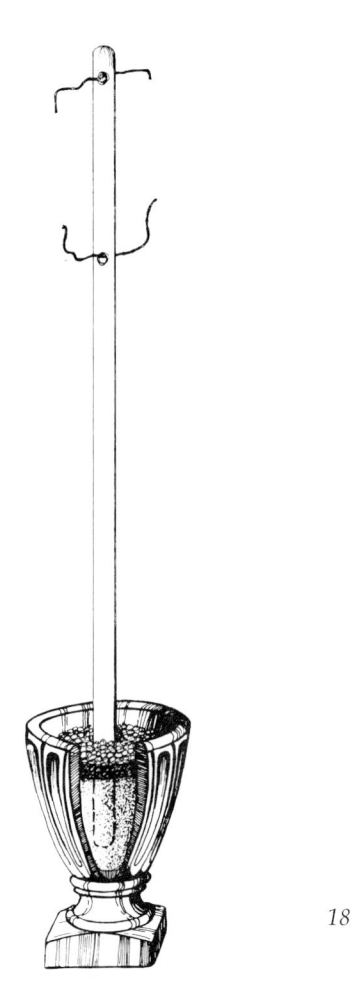

17   Drill small holes through the dowelling rod or broom handle before setting it in sand and concrete.

18   When the concrete has set, the soaked Oasis, wrapped in cling film, is impaled on the rod and enclosed in wire netting, which is fastened with reel wire through the holes.

17

18

very sparingly first to give a protective light cover; when this has hardened the subsequent applications can be more generous.

The tree is now ready to be made up with artificial or fresh plant material.

Other Christmas tips

Polyfilla can be used to secure the wire stems for a traditional mass arrangement. The Christmas table design in colour plate 11 has Polyfilla heaped into 7.5 cm (3 in.) plastic plant pot saucers. The saucers were painted silver first, before the Polyfilla was put in and the flowers were arranged. This makes for very stable arrangements which are easy to store and lovely to give as presents.

Wreaths

Festive door wreaths
In ancient Egypt, Greece and Rome, long before Christ's birth, wreaths and garlands were made for festivals. Often these were hung on doors, so the seeds of this custom were sown many thousands of years ago. We know that door wreaths were adopted in a big way nearer to our own times, when the capital of Virginia Colony, Williamsburg, was reconstructed in 1928 and made to appear as it was in Colonial America. This revival was an inspiration to us in this country and we have copied their

beautiful door wreaths which have become an accepted Christmas feature.

The quickest way of making a traditional wreath is to acquire a wreath frame from a florist. These come in different sizes, but one measuring 25.5 cm (10 in.) across is a convenient diameter for most doors.

Wreaths made on frames, using fresh plant material

METHOD ONE
- Get some sphagnum moss from a florist's shop or garden centre and soak it well.
- Squeeze out the excess moisture and bandage it onto the frame with strips of thin polythene or cling film about 5 cm (2 in.) wide.
- The layer of moss should be 5 cm (2 in.) wide too. The strong wires of the frame will support the moss, but you must bind it on tightly.
- The wreath is now ready for the plant material. Make holes for the stems with a sharp stick of suitable diameter.

METHOD TWO
- Soak a block of Oasis before cutting into pieces 7.5 cm long x 5 cm wide x 3.5 cm deep (3 x 2 x 1½ in.).
- Place the pieces of Oasis on a length of cling film leaving 2.5

WINTER FLOWERS AND CHRISTMAS DECORATIONS

cm (1 in.) between each block of foam.
- Fold the cling film round the Oasis before wiring the spaces between the blocks. The result is like a string of sausages.
- Place the 'sausages' around the wreath frame, making sure the frame supports the 'sausages', and wire them to the frame. Insert the foliage in the same way as is described for the sphagnum moss wreath above. Artificial fruits, plastic or silk Christmas roses, baubles and cones can be added to the fresh material, including bows and tails of ribbon.

Alternative door decorations

Decoration on a round rush mat
This is a quickly-made hanging decoration.
Choose a mat of not less than 20 cm (8 in.) diameter. Wire together a collection of artificial evergreens and/or glittery material, fruits and cones. Attach these slightly above, and to one side, of the mat's centre with thin wire threaded through the mat. Finish with ribbon bows and tails and a loop for hanging.

An alternative method to this is to wire a square of dry Oasis about 5 x 5 cm x 2.5 cm deep (2 x 2 x 1 in.) to the mat, slightly above and off centre. Protect and strengthen the Oasis with a small piece of 2.5 cm (1 in.) wire netting, threading fine wire attached to the wire netting through to the back of the mat and

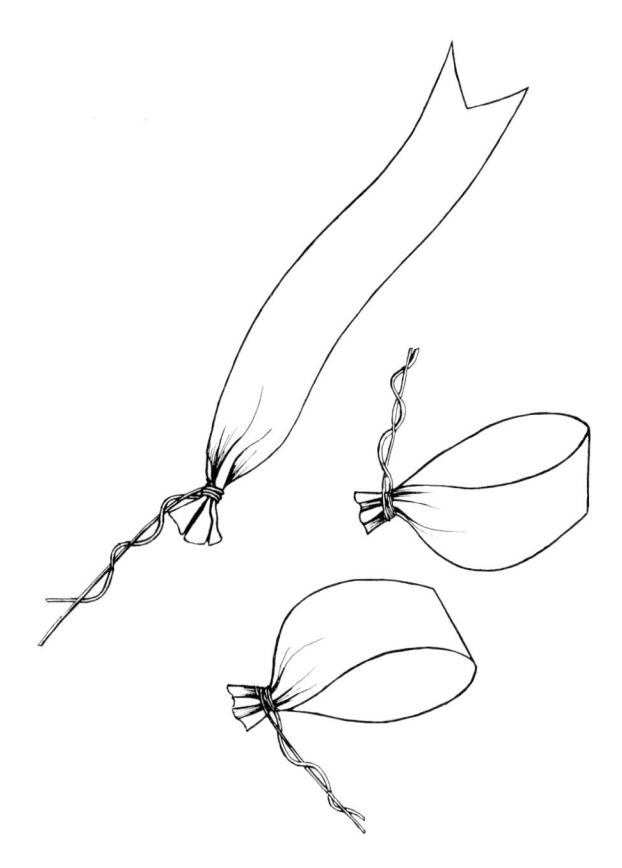

19   *Attach bows and tails of ribbon to topiary trees and wreaths.*

fastening it firmly. The plant material can then be arranged in the Oasis. This method gives a design with greater depth than the one above. Finish with ribbon tails and bows.

The coat hanger decoration
This is another inexpensive and easy way of making a door decoration which could be used for any festive event such as a christening or wedding, using appropriate plant material. It takes longer pieces of foliage than either the mats or wreaths.

The foundation is a taped wire coat hanger, bent as illustrated on page 61 to get rid of the 'shoulder' shape.
- Wrap a piece of wet Oasis in cling film (for fresh material), or cut a piece of dry Oasis (for artificial material), measuring 10 x 10 x 5 cm deep (4 x 4 x 2 in.). Wire the pack of Oasis to the coat hanger under the hook.
- Begin by putting the longest pieces of plant material into the Oasis, using a sharp stick to make a hole in the cling film.
- Wire these first long bits of foliage to the coat hanger to prevent them from slipping. Then work towards the centre with shorter lengths of foliage until the entire hanger and Oasis are covered.
- Cones and/or baubles can be wired and attached and ribbon added below the centre of the Oasis.
- The completed decoration should be an elegant 'C' shape.

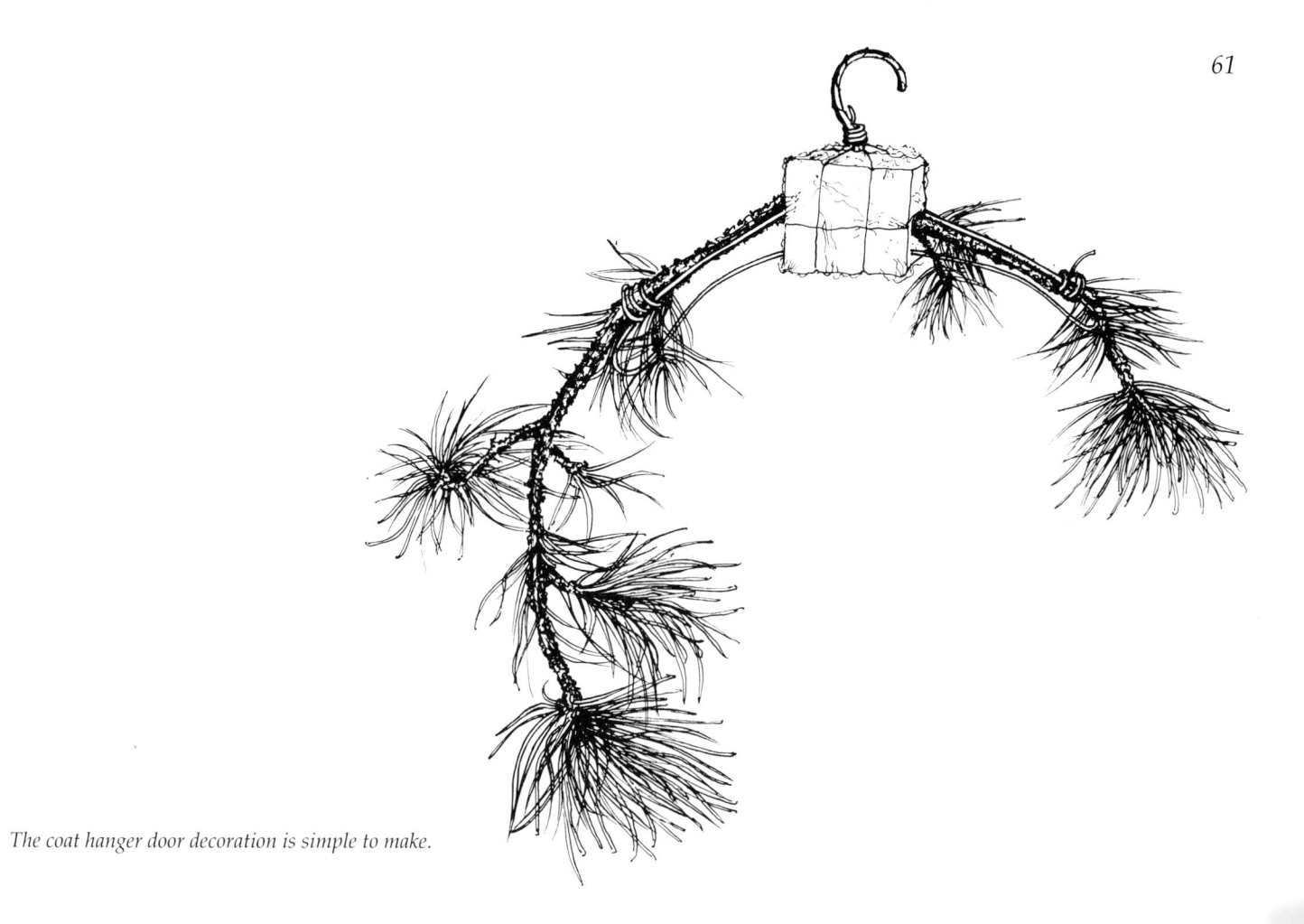

20 *The coat hanger door decoration is simple to make.*

Artificial door ring
If all the component parts of a door decoration are to be of artificial material buy a polystyrene ring; they are made in various sizes. It can be trimmed with ribbon wrapped around it, and clusters of plastic or silk plant material can be added.

Woody-stemmed or hay rings
Wreath bases made of hay bound with wire are a fairly new introduction, and also very pretty. Craft shops also have wreaths made of tightly-bound circles of 'French' broom. When the base is made of natural plant material less decoration is needed. The wreath in colour plate 12 is made from clematis stems – honeysuckle stems would serve the same purpose. There is no thick wire core in the wreath as the clematis stems are quite strong, but wire is bound round a few times to hold the strands of stem in place and is almost invisible.

   This kind of wreath is easier to make if you have a garden, but hedgerows do provide all kinds of twig materials, and a craft shop may supply the 'French' broom circle.

CHRISTMAS GARLANDS AND SWAGS

Choose 2 mm gauge plastic-covered wire for the 'backbone' of a curved garland. Cut a length to fit the place where it will be hung, remembering to allow for the curve when measuring. Tape the entire length of the wire with floral tape; this will give it a tacky surface to which the individually-taped pieces of plant material will readily adhere. If you wish to make a vertical swag use a plant-pot cane and, similarly, cover it with tape. (Both 2 mm gauge wire and the plant-pot cane can be obtained from a hardware shop.)

The plant material must first be assembled so that each piece has its own stem reduced to the minimum. Everything is given a wire stem which is then taped. When all the pieces have been prepared they are put onto the 'backbone'. This is done by pressing the two tacky surfaces together: press the individually-wired bits of plant material to the tacky wire or cane.

- Leave plenty of 'play' in each piece so that it is not clamped closely to its 'backbone'. None of the pieces is wired onto the 'backbone'; instead, secure them with a few twists of tape.
- Cut away any unwanted wire stem. The back of the garland or swag should be smooth and clear as all pieces are put on at the front. If plenty of 'play' is left in the wire stems a certain amount of rearranging can be done if necessary. Things look better when they are taped on in groups, but attach each member of a group separately.
- On completion spray the entire garland or swag gold or silver for Christmas.

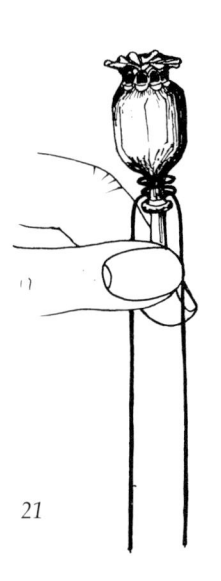

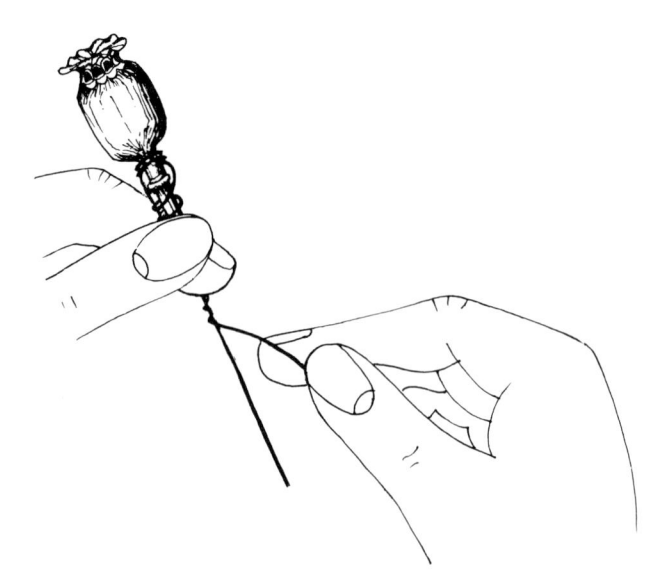

21 Reduce the length of the stem, leaving enough for wiring a false wire stem onto it. Finish by taping the false stem.

22 Dried seedheads etc. look best when they are taped on to the 'backbone' in groups, though each member of a group is attached separately.

1 Anemones and snowdrops
Three bunches of anemones in a Bristol blue jug make a richly coloured group. The mechanics are simply a piece of crumpled wire-netting. These flowers dislike Oasis but last well in water. Four bunches of snowdrops in an assortment of small containers and standing on a piece of perspex.

◁

2 (*Left*) A piece of dried prickly pear gives height, interesting shape and texture and so makes more of the five daffodils. The base leaves are silk and have been wired and taped. The base gives balance but also helps to unite the wood and the flowers.
(*Right*) The tulips are *Gregii* 'Corsage' and the foliage is glycerined beech and ruscus. Both foliages have their stems taped to protect them from the water. The mechanics are a pinholder in the bottom of the jug and a piece of 2.5cm (1in.) wire-netting.

3 A bare branch has been given silk blossom, so it can be used time and again. Here it is accompanied by five white tulips—'White Triumphator'—which have opened wide in the warmth of the room and are showing their stamens. The base leaves are silk, the moss was bought at a garden centre and the slate base came from Cumberland.

▷▷

4 A pot-et-fleur of easy to grow house plants in a 30.48cm wide×12.70cm deep (12×4in.) plastic container. The container has been painted a soft matt greeny-grey. The polyanthus are planted in the compost, but the tulips are in a pinholder in a shallow tin.

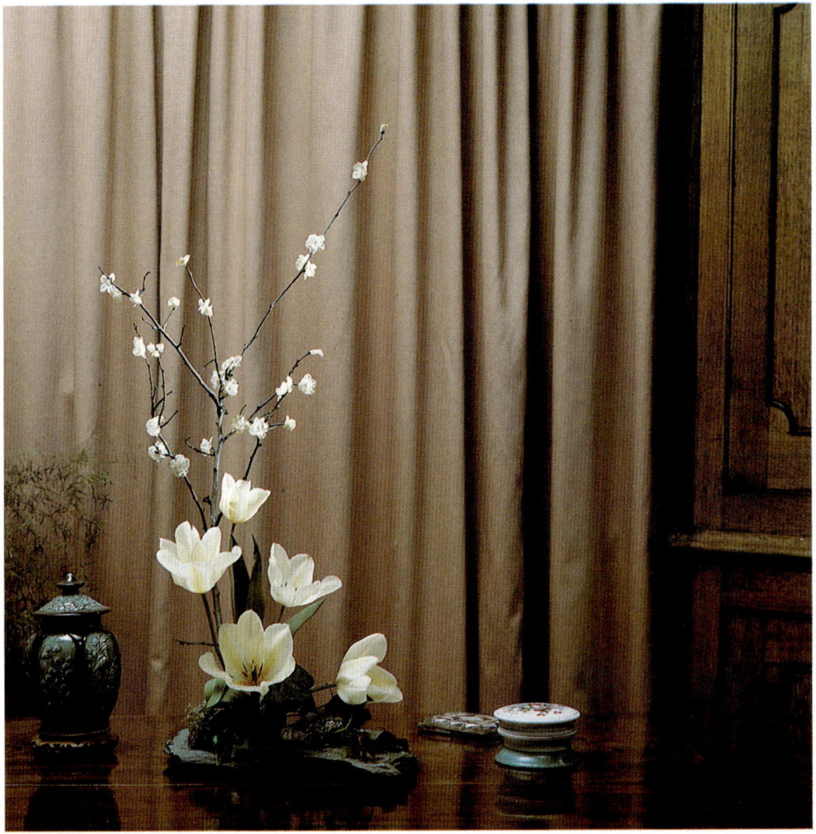
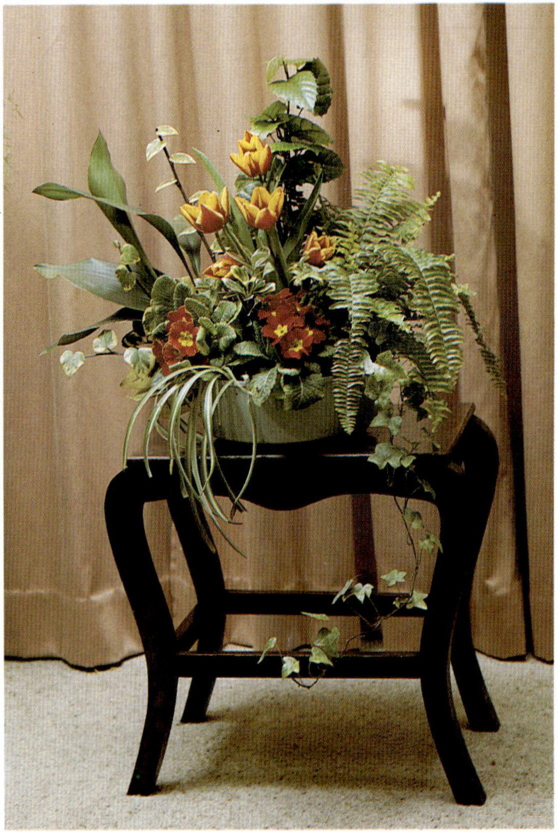

△

5 (*Left*) The little pink 'Doris' is usually available from June well into the autumn. Here it looks very summery with gypsophila in a white container. For the mechanics a pinholder covered with wire-netting is used.

(*Right*) Cornflowers are amongst the earliest annuals to flower. Two mixed bunches have been made into a double design, placed in small jam-jars, which each have a twist of wire-netting in them. To unite the two placements they have matching 'pop-over' covers and base.

◁

6 Three mixed coloured bunches of larkspur and three small pink roses make two entirely different arrangements. The raised design is conventional in shape but the separation of the colours and the absence of foliage are not.

The raised container holds a sprog—made firm with Oasis fix—and a cube of soaked Oasis strengthened with Oasis tape. It stands 3.75cm (1½in.) above the container's rim to allow some downward flow of material.

In the basket there is a small tin for Oasis which is covered with a cap of wire-netting. Reel wire has been fixed to the outside of the wire-netting and then threaded through the basket weave and fastened underneath.

▷

7 The apples, pears and cherries are real and are there to be eaten. The roses are real too and are in a concealed tin of water with a pinholder in it. The grapes and leaves are artificial. This sort of simple grouping is very quick to do, but makes a party atmosphere out of very little.

◁
8 The tea pot is old and beautiful but has a crack so a plastic container has been fitted into it for Oasis. The campanula and 'Iceberg' roses came from the market; the three pink flowers are silk. The only foliage is a spray of house ivy.

◁
9 Nerines in a modern glass container. These blooms have become easily available over the last few years, and flower from late September until Christmas. There is a twist of wire-netting in the top of the vase.

▷

10 The cherub supports a little shelf which makes a wonderful place for flowers. Dried *Statice dumosum*, helipterums, helichrysums and tansy have been arranged in dry Oasis to make a winter decoration for a staircase.

11 The Christmas arrangement would make a good table centre. It is an example of a design using permanent mechanics because the stems are in Polyfilla, which fills two 3.75cm (1.5in.) plant pot saucers. The plastic plant material must be arranged before the plaster begins to set. Two of the slender candles were also put into the plaster; the others have their own small holders.

12 A selection of simple Christmas decorations. The taller tree has a dowelling rod fixed into a large cream carton onto which three polystyrene balls—graduated in size—have been threaded. These have been decorated with artificial holly, red and gold fruits and gilded cones. The trunk of the smaller tree is made from a house plant cane. The larger door wreath on the left has a base of twisted clematis stems; the fruits and holly are artificial. The second hanging decoration has been made on a rush mat with entirely artificial material.

23 When all the pieces have been prepared they are put onto the 'backbone' by pressing the two tacky surfaces together.

5
Pot-et-fleur

POT-ET-FLEUR

The name pot-et-fleur is that given to a collection of growing (rooted) house plants assembled together in one large bowl with the optional addition of cut flowers. The stems of the cut flowers are held in a pinholder in a small container of water, which is then set amongst the plants. More than one container can be used if desired.

If I lived in a flat or some place without a garden a pot-et-fleur would be an absolute necessity. I have a garden which is well-stocked with shrubs especially chosen for flower arranging, but I still have two pots-et-fleur as I like them so much. They are almost trouble-free; they are easy to 'dress up' when flowers are abundant or when there is a special occasion, and accommodating enough to make do with three large flowers or none at all during the lean months. This means of decoration does not quite fulfil the flower arranger's creative urge but it is a most satisfactory second best.

WHICH PLANTS TO USE

Some knowledge of the requirements of the plants to use is helpful, and will prevent you from making mistakes. Specimens should be chosen which will flourish in similar conditions: the same temperature, humidity, amounts of water, light and soil. The plants placed as they are, in close juxtaposition, help to provide one another with a certain amount of humidity as they transpire together and they usually thrive in a pot-et-fleur more satisfactorily than as single specimens dotted around the room. As the charm of a good pot-et-fleur lies in the variety of heights, habits of growth, leaf shapes, colours and textures, there is a wide choice of subjects, but your choice is governed by the temperature and conditions in the room for which the collection is intended. Nearly all plants – apart from those which grow in arid places such as cacti and succulents – need some humidity; modern central heating can be very drying. Syringing the plants' leaves only overcomes this to a small degree.

All designs, whether of cut flowers or grouped pot plants, need to look harmonious. The container should be of a colour and texture that does not dominate the plants. Too many leaf colours and fussy leaf shapes will give a muddled, uncontrolled effect, whilst subtle repetition of colour and shape will result in an integrated collection that appears happily linked together.

CONSTRUCTION

There are two ways of making a pot-et-fleur. For the first method the plants are taken out of their pots and replanted in a large container in John Innes No. 2 compost. Using the second method, the various plants are assembled within the large container, grouped as though growing but left in their individual pots. Both ways have their advantages and disadvantages. Method one gives a completely natural effect, but if a plant does not thrive and has to be taken out and replaced there is a certain amount of disturbance to some of the other roots. Also all the plants have to be watered simultaneously. Method two allows a pot to be taken out without disturbance to its companions and also permits some individual watering; the chief snag with this is that the pots are not easy to camouflage.

The container

The container or bowl should never be less than 10 cm (4 in.) deep. Where the plants are to go into the compost, a deeper one is even better. With the second method it will be the depth of the container that will help to hide the pots so a shallow one is no use. Old washhand-stand bowls are much sought after for the planted groups, but there is a wide selection of suitable containers at the garden centres, and inexpensive plastic ones can be given a coat of paint, textured with sand or plaster or a specially made mixture and improved beyond recognition for very little cost. Earthy colours blend best with growing plants: try a coat of a mid-grey undercoat followed by the application of a little mid-green mixed into the grey before it has had a chance to dry. The surface is more attractive if it is not too uniform in colour. Car body spray can be applied in a few quick bursts after the basic colour has dried and this will highlight any relief on the container.

Method one

Materials: A large container of a minimum depth of 10 cm (4 in.). Drainage material: pebbles, broken crocks, builders' rubble or gravel for drainage, obtainable from a garden centre or builder. John Innes compost No. 2, sold in bags at garden centres. A few pieces of charcoal to keep the compost sweet, a hardware store or garden centre will have this.

(1) Prick holes in the bag of compost with a fork and submerge it in a bowl of water for about ten minutes, then tip the contents of the bag into a bowl or bucket and mix thoroughly, making sure it is uniformly moist but *NOT* wet.
(2) Place a 2.5 – 5 cm (1 – 2 in.) layer of drainage material in the bottom of the container. This will allow excess water to drain away from the compost and plant roots. Plants dislike waterlogged soil and will die if left in such conditions.
(3) Mix into the drainage material a few pieces of charcoal.
(4) Put in a layer of compost, but do not fill the container.
(5) Water the plants to be transferred to the compost first so that they come out of the pots easily. Turn them upside-down and

squeeze them if plastic – or tap them briskly if terracotta. Hold your hand so that the first and second fingers are around the stem; the plants should fall from the pots into your waiting hand.

(6) Arrange the tallest plants towards the back of the container, the bushy ones next and trailers so that they drape over the rim. Leave a space towards the front-middle for a tin to hold a pinholder. When the plants are attractively placed fill in the holes with the compost, firming it down gently. Do not over-fill the container – there must be at least 2.5 cm (1 in.) between the top of the compost and the rim so that the plants can be watered.

24 *Method one for making a pot-et-fleur.*

The newly-planted bowl
Your pot-et-fleur will take a few weeks to settle down and begin to grow. If plants have been chosen that are good companions there should be no problems at all. The tin containing the pinholder – one of 5 cm (2 in.) is a sensible size – should be fitted into the compost and hidden by foliage. The cut flowers chosen for inclusion in the pot-et-fleur must be of a suitable scale to go with the display: large dahlias, chrysanthemums and gladioli all look good, as do lilies. Don't fan out the flowers but concentrate them in the centre, zig-zagging them in a line of descending height. Remember to fill up the tin with water daily, but only water the compost when it really needs it – more plants are killed by over-watering than by anything else.

When flowering plants are included in the pot-et-fleur, additional cut blooms may not be necessary. A collection containing flowering plants will need more attention than one of foliage plants because they must have a good light, possibly direct sunlight, if they are to flourish. Variegated leaves also require a strong light if they are to keep their variegation.

Method two
Similar materials are needed for method two as for method one, except that peat can be substituted for the John Innes No. 2 compost. Also a 2.5 cm (1 in.) layer of crocks is enough for the

drainage. You may need inverted plant pots to lift some of the plants to the required level.
- Make a firm layer of drainage crocks and add a few bits of charcoal.
- Place the potted plants on top of the crocks, supporting them on empty pots if necessary, until they make an attractive group. Some small pots of trailing growers will be needed to cover the rim of the container. The taller pots should be hidden by the foliage of those placed in front of them. Make a position for the pinholder tin.

25   *Method two for making a pot-et-fleur.*

Other pot-et-fleur ideas

Other components can be added to a pot-et-fleur to give extra interest: e.g., dried wood, stones, shells or a figurine.

A pot-et-fleur of succulents
It is surprising that more people do not like these plants, especially as they love a dry atmosphere and are the answer to problems of dryness caused by central heating. Small cut flowers are such a pretty addition when placed amongst them in a tiny container – the perfect way to use the small spring flowers. A succulent is a plant with thick fleshy leaves which is happy in arid surroundings. There are hundreds of plants in this group that need practically no attention, though they must have sunlight and good drainage, the latter achieved by making a compost of two parts John Innes No. 2 and one part sharp sand or grit. Most of the succulents belong to the family *Crassulaceae* and all require minimum watering except when the flower buds are forming when they need a little more moisture.

Choosing succulents
The sansevieria or 'Mother-in-law's tongue' is the tallest for this purpose and would go into the back of the bowl. Aloes, crassula and kalanchoës are of medium height and there are hundreds of low-growing, knobbly and rosette-producing plants amongst

the sedums, echeverias and sempervivums. All these are very easily propagated – just detach one of the fleshy leaves, allow it to dry for a day or two and then lay it on the compost where it will send out roots from the stem end and eventually form a tiny new plant.

Maintaining pot-et-fleur

Every established pot-et-fleur will need feeding during the growing season. There are many proprietary fertilizers on the market for this purpose. Always read the instructions on the packet or bottle and don't be tempted to give the plants an extra dose. Also look out for pests and diseases: greenfly, whitefly, red spider and scale insects are the commonest. There are pesticides and fungicides available for the treatment of all troubles.

It is impossible to overemphasize the importance of selecting plants that will live happily together. Although plants – like people – adapt to new surroundings amazingly well, it takes time, and with a pot-et-fleur success is more likely when considerable care is taken over the choice. Buy from a reputable firm whose labels will give instructions about maintenance. Garden centres usually have one area for plants requiring a high temperature and another for those that are less delicate. It seems safe to put together specimens from the same area, but the requirements of soil, light and water must be ascertained.

Never feel that a sickly plant must be nursed. It is better to get rid of ailing things and replace them with new healthy ones.

Remember to select some plants for height, others for their bushy growth habit and some for their ability to trail over the container's rim. The edge will be softened by the trailers, and the stems of the tallest hidden by the bushy growers.

Here is a list of plants and their special needs which may be useful for pot-et-fleur arrangements. The plants whose requirements are described as 'moderate' are those that do not need brilliant light, much heat or a constant supply of water.

Plants to give height	Requirements and care
Asparagus plumosus	Moderate
Aspidistra elatior	Easy
Asplenium nidus	Good humidity
Cissus antarctica	No direct sunlight
C. rhombifolia	
Cleyera japonica	Moderate
Cordyline terminalis	Moderate
Dracaena – various	Humidity, warmth but no direct sunlight
Fatshedera lizei	Moderate
Grevillea robusta	Moderate
Hedera helix – various	Moderate
To be trained on to a frame	
Howeia belmoreana	Moderate
H. forsteriana	
Rhoicissus capensis	Moderate

Plants for the middle of a pot-et-fleur	Requirements and care
Asplenium bulbiferum	High humidity
Begonia rex	High humidity
Dieffenbachia – various	Warmth and humidity. Medium light
Euonymus japonicus 'Argenteo-variegatus'	Good light but cool conditions
Ficus rubiginosa 'Variegata'	Moderate
Fittonia verschaffeltii	Medium light, moisture and humidity
Glechoma hederacea	Moderate
Nephrolepis exaltata – and various	Humidity
Peperomia obtusifolia	Humidity
P. argyreia	
P. griseo-argentea	
Pteris – various	Humidity

Plants that trail but which also have some height	Requirements and care
Asparagus asparagoides	Moderate but needing plenty of water
A. sprengeri	
Begonia foliosa	Warmth, moderate humidity and water. No direct sunlight
Chlorophytum comosum 'Variegatum'	Moderate warmth and water. No direct sunlight
Hedera helix – various To be allowed to trail	Moderate
Pellaea rotundifolia	Tolerates low light and is moderate in every way

Peperomia serpens	Warmth, medium humidity but no direct sunlight
Saxifrage stolonifera	Good drainage, moderate in every way
Senecio rowleyanus	Warmth, dry conditions
S. herreianus	
Scindapsus pictus	Warmth
Tolmiea menziesii	Moderate
Zebrina purpusii	Warmth, moderate
Z. pendula 'Quadricolour'	

INDOOR BULBS

A way of gardening on a limited scale is to plant bulbs in pots during the autumn and bring them into the house to flower earlier than they would outdoors. Below are a few points to ensure success.

• *Buy the best quality you can find* and choose those specially prepared for forcing, for these will have been kept in the most suitable conditions so that they will come into flower at the expected time. Bulbs have their own store of food and also contain the embryo flowers and leaves; all they require is the correct rooting medium and water.

• *Anything may be used as a container* as long as the depth and width are right for the number and size of the bulbs to be planted. There must be enough depth to allow for root development. Daffodil and narcissi bulbs can be planted in layers – staggered – in deep containers. It does not matter if the bulbs touch each other on either side.

- *If the container has no drainage holes* a proprietary brand of bulb fibre is best: this is a mixture of peat, coconut fibre, charcoal and oyster shell – the last two keep the mixture sweet. You will need to moisten it well before it is used, but take care not to over-water it or the developing roots will get water-logged. After soaking the peat-based fibre you can squeeze it by hand to extract excess moisture.
- *When the container has drainage holes* John Innes No. 2 compost may be used. Moisten this too before planting the bulbs.

Planting hyacinths, daffodils and other bulbs

Gravel makes a rooting medium for hyacinths and the earliest daffodils such as the little Grand Soleil d'Or and Paperwhite grandiflora. There is no nourishment to be had from the gravel, but the bulbs contain all that they need. Care must be taken when growing bulbs in gravel not to over-water. Do not let the base of the bulbs be constantly in contact with the water, for this will cause them to rot. Let only the roots be in the water and not the bulb.

John Innes No. 2 and special bulb fibre are sold in bags and can be simply moistened by making a few holes in the bag with a household fork and then putting it into a bowl of water for ten minutes. The moisture content of the soil or fibre is correct if it crumbles slightly when you first squeeze it and then release it.

Daffodils and hyacinths can be planted with their noses protruding from the compost. Cover other bulbs completely. Do not overfill the container with compost; it should be well below the rim to allow for watering. Do not pack the compost down too tightly or the penetrating roots will lift the bulbs.

Once the bulbs are planted they should be put into a cool, dark place to encourage root development and leaf formation. They should be checked weekly to make sure the compost does not dry out.

When the leaves are 2.5 – 5 cm (1 – 2 in.) high, gradually introduce them to the light by putting the containers first into a dim light and then, by degrees, into stronger light until they may go on to a window-sill; this process should take about two weeks. A final temperature of 10° C (50°F) is ideal. Many bulbs will need some support, twigs or a stick; these should be put in early so that the leaves grow around them. The compost looks more attractive when covered with moss; failing woodland moss, reindeer moss is equally acceptable and can be bought at florists' shops or garden centres.

It is advisable not to mix different-coloured hyacinths in the same container, for they will probably not come into flower

together. When a succession of flowers is wanted bring the bowls one at a time into greater heat. The time to plant is in August and September. Not every spring-flowering bulb does well in the house, but the following can usually be relied upon:
- All hyacinths specially prepared for the house.
- The dwarf irises *I. reticulata* and *I. histriodes* are rewarding.
- Chionodoxas and scillas are pretty but do not always flower together.
- All crocuses, apart from the yellow ones, will force.
- Out of the vast number of tulips choose from the early single and doubles – these seem to do especially well.

NB It is best to avoid the tallest daffodils as they tend to fall about because of their height.

6
Fruit, foliage and flowers

THE USE OF FRUIT AS DECORATION

Most households today have a supply of fruit each week which can be used for decorative purposes before it is eventually consumed. It is a hazard that the arrangement will diminish as the days go by unless there are a few spares in the background, or the odd silk flower or bunch of plastic grapes to fill in the holes! Fruit is especially suitable for table and sideboard designs, and when the dining area is in the kitchen vegetables can be brought into the arrangements too.

The Egyptians

The shape and colour and texture of fruit and vegetables is very beautiful; a fact much appreciated by past civilizations. In ancient Egypt, offering-tables, vases and trays were piled with a mixture of fruit, vegetables and flowers. They used various plant materials with formal symmetry, an orderliness characteristic of the race. The wide collarettes made by the Egyptians for funerals were of leaves, fruit, flowers and beads and were elaborate adornments.

The classical world

After the Egyptians, both the Greeks and Romans filled baskets and cornucopias with flowers and fruit, but in a far less stylized manner. They also made wreaths and garlands, binding the plant material onto vine or fig stems, or sometimes sewing it together. One cannot help wondering how the flowers and leaves were conditioned to stop them from wilting in the hot southern sunshine, or did they always flag by evening having served their purpose? The Greeks had a ceremonial staff called a *thyrsus* which was carried at festivals of Dionysus; this was decorated with ivy, berries and grapes and topped with a large pine cone symbolizing the apple of the pine. A swag of fruit and flowers called an *encarpa* was made to embellish sculptures and paintings, and head wreaths were worn to celebrate various achievements.

Italian Renaissance paintings show many such decorations inspired by the ancients. Flowers were seldom seen in profusion at this period, but there were always plenty of leaves, massed thickly, with the fruit grouped amongst them and a sprinkling of flowers, as though growing in a meadow.

The Dutch school

During the seventeenth and eighteenth centuries the Dutch/Flemish artists placed fruit below the imposing vases holding flowers of every season and painted them together. The fact that the fruit was used symbolically did nothing to detract from its effectiveness. The symbolism of the period is fascinating to study: it was known as the 'Vanitas' theme, a reminder of the vanities of this world. The artists painted damaged or half-peeled fruit, leaves with holes in them caused by insects, and marred flowers, all symbolizing worldly evils. The shining drops of water clinging to the flowers and leaves were reminders of the transience of life. Objects such as jewellery, dice and books represented the worldly interests of men; whilst ears of corn, birds' nests containing eggs, fluttering moths and butterflies were there to remind the viewer of the resurrection.

As the eighteenth century progressed these religious allusions on the canvases grew fewer until they eventually disappeared altogether; the fruit, however, continued to be painted for its beauty and has remained one of the most prominent components of still-life art.

The British and fruit

In the important country houses of England the fruit for dessert was assiduously arranged with leaves in great piles by the head gardener. These compositions frequently took the place of flowers on the dining tables. There is nothing original in arranging fruit; the wonder is that it isn't done more often.

In the greengrocer's window, on the street barrows and market stalls even the commonest fruits and vegetables are stacked with precision, the demarkation line between the different things being crisp and clear. Abroad the stalls are even more attractive because of the unfamiliarity of many items and the abundance and cheapness of some fruits and vegetables which are luxuries in this country.

However I always feel a twinge of dissatisfaction, something isn't quite as it ought to be – this stems from my longing to add leaves to the pyramids to emphasise their brilliance with the contrast of plain green. In the home this contrast can easily be had with the use of silk foliage if fresh is at a premium. There are also plenty of realistic artificial fruits and vegetables to buy. High on the list of excellent reproductions come the bunches of plastic grapes; the best, of course, are the most expensive, but these are so clever that I would not think of putting fresh grapes into an arrangement unless it was for a competition where disqualification would follow the use of anything artificial.

ARRANGING FRUIT

The mechanics for fruit need to be completely firm – as they do for every design – but as fruit is heavy it must be made extra secure. When fresh flowers and foliage are combined with plastic fruit the living materials must be in water, either in a hidden pinholder tin or in wet foam. Obviously, if silk flowers and leaves take the place of fresh a water supply is not needed,

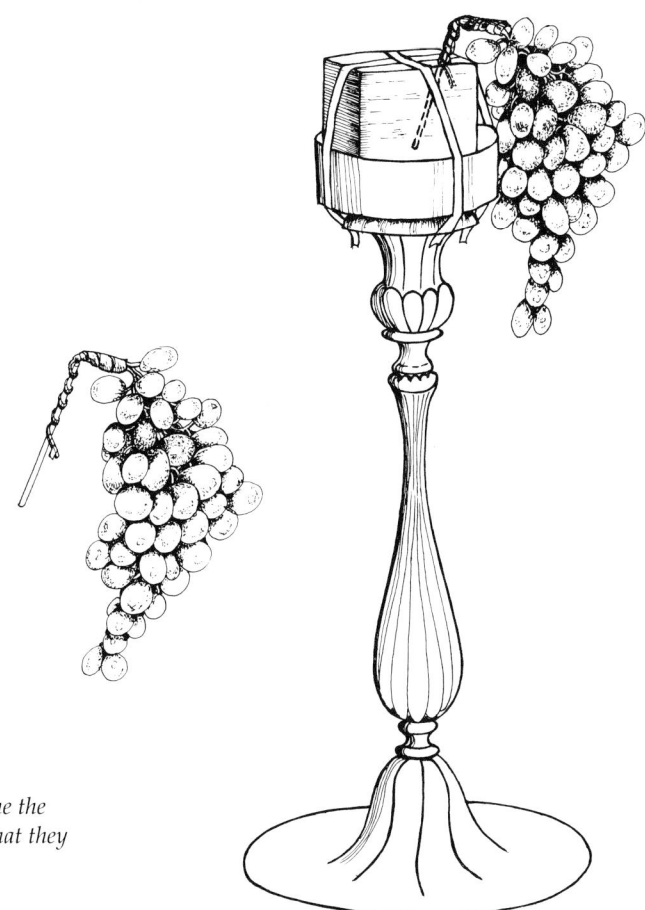

26 High on the list of excellent reproductions come the bunches of plastic grapes. Wire them to a stick so that they go into the Oasis easily.

but some mechanics are necessary to help the arranger fix the stems and vary the height of the materials, be they flowers, fruit, foliage or vegetables. Nothing spoils an arrangement more than a flat and level collection of forms. Stems of silk flowers can be wired to give more height, or cut to different lengths, but wooden skewers, cocktail sticks and wires are needed for fruit to achieve ths variety. Wires used carefully need not spoil the fruit.

Soft fruits, such as strawberries and raspberries, are best presented on leaves as they are in France, Switzerland and Italy, to be eaten there and then. They are not really suitable for using as an important part of an arrangement, except for the odd bunch of half-ripe fruit. Crab apples, cherries and red currants can play a part in decorations; clustered together and wired into place, they make more impact than scattered around. They are much easier to handle than strawberries and raspberries.

Nuts of every kind should also be grouped and need to be wired. To do this successfully drill a hole through the nuts with the greatest care; use a vice to hold the nuts, or your fingers may be at risk. Nuts may be made into more permanent decorations by being glued to some sort of framework such as a cone or ring. They look lovely when sprayed with gold or any other metallic aerosol, which enhances their texture.

Acorns, gourds, beech mast and horsechestnuts – with or without their cases – are not for man's consumption. The various

27 *Nothing spoils an arrangement more than a flat collection of forms; fruit depends on wooden skewers, cocktail sticks and wires to achieve variety in height and depth.*

FRUIT, FOLIAGE AND FLOWERS 87

28 Supports for a pineapple.

29 Cherries clustered together, and wired into place before being taped make more impact than when they are scattered around.

cones and seed heads are all fruits and many can be found in the countryside or under trees in parks during the autumn. Some garden centres and florists will sell certain seed heads ready-dried. When ornamental gourds are to be dried, remember they will take a very long time indeed in a constantly warm place. When they feel as light as air they are ready to store; at this point they can be sealed with a clear varnish which will exclude the air and make them last longer. I have had some for many years protected this way. Any preserved dried plant material may be treated in like manner but it must be considered whether a gloss finish is desirable for everything. Glossy surfaces are sadly missing from the dried category of plant material.

CONTAINERS FOR FRUIT ARRANGEMENTS

It isn't essential to arrange fruit in a container but without one a base is a necessity, otherwise the fruit simply looks as though it has been dropped onto the table top. The base can be a raffia or bamboo mat, or a board such as a cake board covered with material to harmonize with the fruit and flowers and the colour scheme of the room. A shallow container is better than a deep one, for depth will swallow some of the fruit and make the mechanics too low. Baskets always look right with fruit or flowers or both. There are so many of these to choose from and

FRUIT, FOLIAGE AND FLOWERS

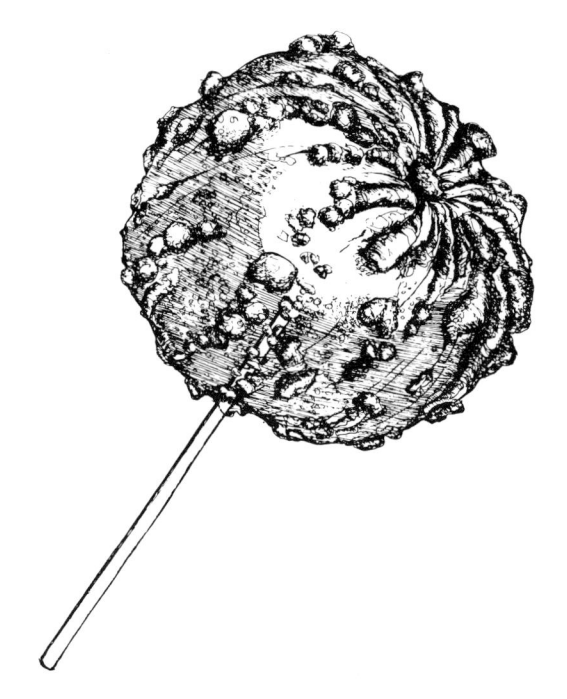

31 *How to wire beech mast before taping.*

30 *The wooden skewer has been glued into the dried gourd.*

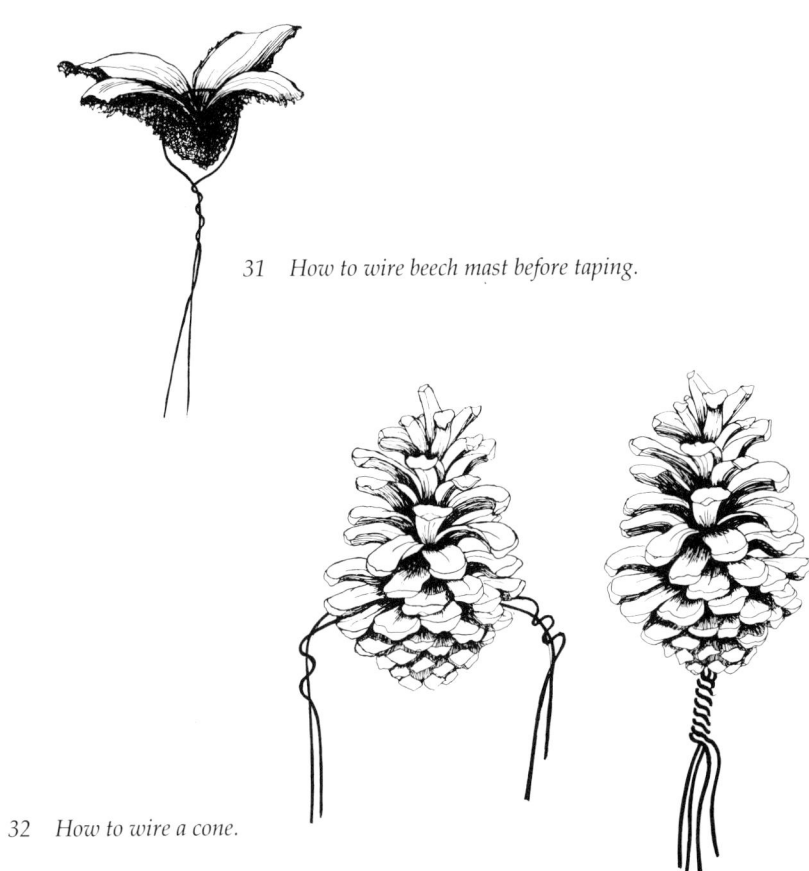

32 *How to wire a cone.*

they cost so little that a basket shop is a rewarding hunting ground. They are suitable for almost any design other than the most sophisticated.

No table decoration should obscure the view of those sitting opposite each other at a formal meal. Unlike the Victorians, who were only supposed to converse with their neighbours, we like to talk to the people sitting facing us. If the design is for a buffet then the fruit and flowers can be as high as you wish because they will be seen by standing guests. For a sideboard the container can be a raised one or not, as wished. The old-fashioned cake stand comes in handy for fruit as it provides a platform for mechanics.

Cake stands will also hold a pyramid of fruit. Mechanics for these used to be made of a pyramid of wood studded with nails at regular intervals, on which the apples – or other fruits – were impaled. This can now be done on Oasis strengthened with wire and supported with a large heavy Oasis holder, for the weight of the fruit is considerable unless smaller things are used, such as crab apples, clementines and kumquats. Remember to use leaves amongst the fruit.

7
Preserving plant material

There are three main ways of preserving plant material: glycerining, drying and pressing. For anyone who enjoys all the peripheral pursuits connected with flower arranging but has little access to a garden, a few preserved leaves and flowers are useful. Leaves are especially important for covering stems in a woody arrangement. They also provide visual base weight and so prevent a top-heavy look.

Silk leaves will serve the same purpose if no preserved ones are at hand, and there is a good assortment of plain ones on sale, of various sizes, that can be wired and taped ready for use.

PRESERVING BY PRESSING

Pressing, as the word implies, results in a two-dimensional shape used for making pictures that will be tightly-held under glass. There cannot be a third dimension although one can be hinted at by the overlapping of the material. Picture making is an excellent occupation for winter evenings and it is a craft that has the advantage of not requiring a lot of space, either for carrying out or storing. Almost any leaves and flowers may be pressed, but the smaller things are more manageable and, to my mind, make the most attractive pictures. The flowers to avoid are the thick and heavy ones, including all succulents. Week by week a few of the flowers brought home from the market can be put between blotting paper and pressed in the pages of an old telephone directory or other heavy book, or even a magazine with a weight on top. This hobby is certainly not expensive, for a proper flower press is not essential, although it is nice to have one, particularly to take on holiday either abroad or to the countryside. Many flowers, leaves and tendrils from the hedgerows are beautiful to press and will add considerable interest to a picture.

- As the object of pressing is to remove all moisture from the leaves and flowers make sure these are dry when picked and put between the blotting paper.
- Select undamaged plant material; there is no point in wasting time and space on imperfect things.
- Press all aspects of the flowers including buds, stems and tendrils, if any, and leaves of various sizes.
- Double and complicated flowers with many stamens need to be taken to pieces and all portions pressed separately; these will be reassembled when put into the picture.
- The press or book must be kept in a dry and slightly warm place. Leave the material in the press for at least three weeks. Once pressed, the flowers and leaves must be kept flat, between layers of either blotting paper or tissues. It is helpful to label the layers so that you don't have a frantic search through the entire collection when you want a certain flower.

Colour retention

The retention of the true colour varies considerably.
- Orange and yellow keep their colour best.
- Green either gradually fades to grey-green or darkens.
- Grey remains constant.
- Red darkens eventually to brown.
- Some pale blues keep their colour well, stronger blues tend to darken.
- Brown is constant.
- White turns cream with time.

However, even when the colours fade, an attractive silhouette remains. It is quite possible to touch up the petals with water-based paint; a drop of washing-up liquid in the paint water helps it to spread smoothly and to adhere. But do remember – if artificial colouring is used on some things in the picture and not on others, the painted pieces will stand out brightly if the others fade, so use paint very sparingly.

PRESERVING WITH GLYCERINE

This method of preservation is for leaves, bracts – which are modified leaves – and seedheads. The advantages of material preserved with glycerine is that it is tough, pliable and sometimes very glossy, the latter being a quality sadly missing with dried things. It can be freshened up by being steamed or even washed in mild detergent and tepid water, but be sure to dry it well if this is done. When not in use, glycerined leaves can be packed away. The colour of the treated material varies between pale cream and dark brown.

Foliage must be mature before it is put into glycerine. It is also important that deciduous leaves should still be taking up water, for towards the autumn a barrier forms between the leaf and its stem so that it can no longer get water passed to it from the root hairs; this causes the leaf to fall. The barrier is known as the abscission layer, and no leaf is capable of absorbing glycerine when this has taken place, so for deciduous foliage mid-June to mid-August is the best time.

(1) The usual proportion is one part of glycerine to two parts water. Put the glycerine into a measuring jug and add two parts of boiling water. Stir well. Never heat glycerine as it is combustible.

(2) Scrape the bark from the bottom two inches of all woody branches and cut upwards for about 2.5 cm (1 in.) so the solution can enter the branches more easily.

(3) Use a really stable vessel to hold the mixture and do not put too much plant material into it as air must be able to circulate. Woody branches can go into the solution whilst it is still quite

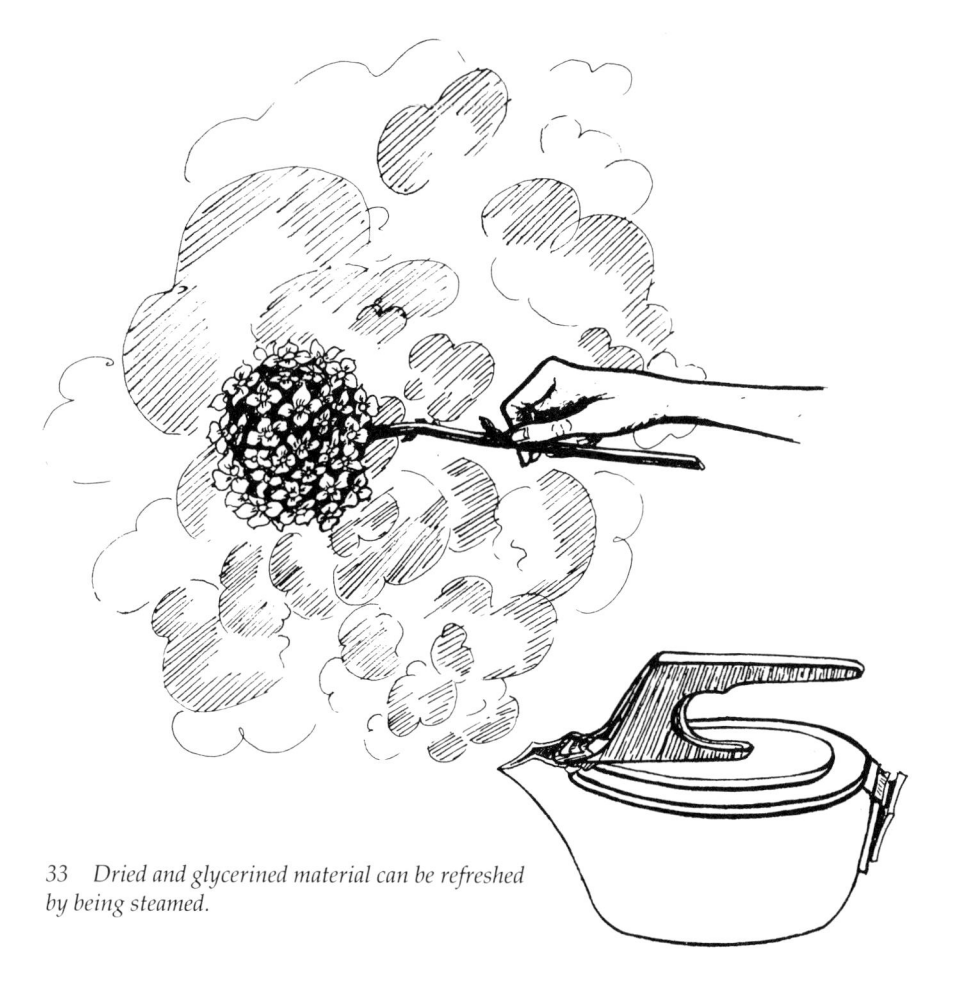

33   Dried and glycerined material can be refreshed by being steamed.

34   Put one part of glycerine into a heat-proof jug and add two parts of boiling water. Stir well.

hot, but wait until it is cold before using it for soft-stemmed things. If the vessel is placed in a good light leaves will turn paler than if it is left in a dark place. Single large leaves may be submerged in the solution; this is necessary for some very thick-leaved subjects and for ferns. A shallow trough will be needed for such material. Usually, the thinner the leaf the faster it will respond to the glycerine.

(4) It is now the custom to leave the plant material in the glycerine long enough for the main veins, or lower bracts, to change colour; this could be anything from three to seven days. It should then be hung upside-down, tied in small bunches and in a good light until the remainder of the leaves have changed colour. This is a far better method than the old one of leaving the material in the solution until it had completely turned colour. Hanging takes up less room and the turnover of material is far greater. This method also prevents 'over-glycerining', the results of which are beads of oily moisture oozing from the leaves.

(5) Store finished material between newspapers which will absorb excess glycerine – if any. The finished things should be kept in a dry atmosphere but not a warm one, for thin leaves eventually wither in heat. Thick leaves will last for years.

PRESERVING BY DRYING

Certain flowers dry without help from us. These are known as the 'immortelles' – a pretty name, I think. They are nearly all annuals and can be found on market stalls and in the florists' shops from July onwards. They are grown especially for drying, and harvested as soon as about one third of the flowers show signs of maturity, with the remainder still buds. They may look unpromising at this stage, but here is the correct way to deal with them.

Take the bunches home and in the case of helichrysums cut off all the flowers including the tiny buds, and push a wire of approximately 0.7 cm (22 gauge) or 0.6 cm (24 gauge) straight into the flower from beneath. The alternative way is to make a small hook at one end of the wire and push the other end through the head of the flower from above. I find the first method perfectly adequate as the wire rusts with the flower's moisture and becomes tightly bonded. The length of the wire stems can be varied: the largest flowers will need the shortest stems, for they will be arranged towards the centre of the designs whilst the smaller flowers need the longest wires, for they will be placed near the perimeter.

Keep all the buds and dry them on a tray. They will expand as they dry and be useful for collage or for three-dimensional

35 *Push a wire straight into the flower head from beneath before it begins to dry. The wire will rust into the flower and will be quite firm. If you want to make doubly sure you can make a small hook at the top.*

pictures in a box frame. Put the wired helichrysums to dry thoroughly in an airy place out of direct sunshine. Direct sunshine will cause the colours to fade.

The pink daisy-like helipterums are cut at a similar stage of their development and are bunched and sold. Do not cut these off the stems but remove the leaves before tying them into bunches and hanging them upside-down to dry, again in an airy place out of direct sunshine. The flowers will continue to grow and open and the slender stems will harden enough to support the almost weightless flowers. If necessary a stem may be given support by being wrapped around with a fine wire – 0.28 cm (32 gauge). Tape the stems when a wire has been added. Use green tape if the helipterums are to be mixed with green foliage, but white tape if they are to be arranged by themselves.

Statice is another plant grown because it dries naturally. There are several species of statice, botanically known as limonium. The most commonly seen is *Limonium sinuatum*, which has a remarkable range of colour: salmon, red, rose, yellow, cream, white, blue and purple. Two other species often used by flower arrangers are *Limonium suworowii*, with spikes of rose-pink flowers, and *Limonium dumosum*, with small white flowers on curving grey-green stems; this latter species is excellent for making topiary trees.

There are other flowers that keep their colour when dried but which rely far more on the skill of the drier for success. The delphinium is one, and its annual form, the larkspur, another. Both need to be hung upside-down in a warm, dry place, out of direct sunshine. Neither should be too far out when this is done. Achillea, echinops and eringium dry easily too but need to be fairly well in flower before they are gathered. They can often be bought ready-dried. The largest proportion of dried material is made up of seedheads. The English ones are on the small side, but reinforced by seedpods and spathes from abroad, which are larger and bolder than our own, a good assortment can be found.

In the British Isles there are plenty of members of the Umbelliferae family familiar to nearly everyone: cow parsley, fennel, wild angelica and the giant hog-weed are some of them. They give us the 'umbrella-spoke'-like material that can be dried in the autumn. Unpicked, they remain on the grass verges of our roadsides throughout the winter and look spectacular when they are whitened by hoar frost. Such an effect can be obtained by spraying and/or glittering the umbels for Christmas arrangements. Most seedheads dry naturally on the plant, which saves a lot of trouble.

Cones, beech mast, acorns (see Chapter 6), along with dried hydrangea heads and the umbels of the Umbelliferae tribe can be lightened in colour in a strong solution of bleach. Try one third bleach to two parts of water, but be prepared to make this mixture stronger. Leave the plant material immersed for half an hour to one hour – according to its toughness. When a satisfactory creamy tint has been reached rinse the material well in cold water and dry it carefully. I am always surprised how well the seemingly fragile things stand up to the strong bleach – only if they are left for a day or more do they begin to disintegrate.

All dried material is brittle and needs care when it is stored.

Drying in desiccants

A different way of drying flowers is to use a desiccant. It results in completely dry flowers that retain their colour and form. The desiccant will absorb all the moisture from the plant material and leave it looking as though it were freshly gathered. Perhaps I should add that it is a process that takes great patience and it is learnt chiefly by trial and error – however, it is an exciting process.

There are several desiccants:

(1) Sand is the cheapest, but it is also the slowest-acting. It must be thoroughly washed and dried before use.

(2) Alum and/or borax from the chemist. Both of these have fine grains and will not mark the petals. They tend to be rather sticky, but they are inexpensive, and many people find them quite satisfactory.

(3) It is possible to experiment with the 'biological' washing powders.
(4) Silica gel is the medium that is most reliable.

Silica gel
If you buy silica gel from a chemist it is usually coarse-grained and will need to be ground down to make a finer powder. There are brands on the market especially for flower arrangers and a good stockist of flower-arranging aids will sell it or be able to tell you where to obtain it. Although the specially-prepared brands are a bit dearer, they are ready for use and will have instructions accompanying them. These prepared crystals will have colour added which fades when they need reactivating, for all desiccants have to be dried out after use in an oven at a temperature of 101°C (250°F) – this takes about half an hour. The crystals get extremely hot during this process so be sure they have cooled before using them again.

There are two important things: do give the flowers fine wire stems BEFORE treating them, having first removed their natural stems; and do follow the instructions. Flowers dried in this manner are very delicate and wiring them after they have been dried is almost impossible. They must be stored in an airtight box and should be arranged under a glass dome, lidded goblet or in a glazed box frame. I have stressed the importance of wiring

36 *Give the flowers fine wire stems before putting them into a desiccant.*

helichrysums before the flower has begun to dry. The same rule applies to flowers dried in a desiccant. It is easy to push a wire into a moist bloom, but impossible to get one into a dried flower without breaking it.

SILK FLOWERS

There has been a rapid escalation in the use of silk flowers during the past ten years or so. Although today there are many realistic, pretty ones, at one time there were lots of rather nasty plastic flowers about too. But now the silk and polyester sort are everywhere and they have to be admired for being so lifelike. They are attractive in shop-window displays, hairdressing salons and lots of overheated places where fresh flowers couldn't last 24 hours. For those without a garden, who have to beg or buy every piece of foliage and each single flower, they must be a godsend. Nothing, however, will ever take the place of the fresh flower, with its changing shape from bud to open bloom.

Silk flowers can pad out an arrangement and make a few fresh flowers go further; they also enable a decoration to be whipped together quickly when unexpected visitors turn up. Most of the silk and polyester flowers are copies of real ones – carnations can be so exact that it is difficult to tell the difference – but there are some which do not pretend to ape the real thing, notably the large cream, tan and brown poppies which look so dramatic when grouped together in a tall container.

It is the plastic stems of the silk flowers that spoil the otherwise excellent workmanship, for they are too stiff and clumsy. It is worth replacing these with wire ones which can be made to bend gracefully and allow a choice in the angling of the head of the flower – an important point. Figs 37 and 38 show you how to wire leaves and stems. The wired stems of both leaves and flowers will often have to be shortened or lengthened according to the design. It would be a good idea to have a collection of prepared material of different lengths. Wires are manufactured in different thicknesses and lengths, and experience will soon enable you to select the correct strength of wire for the size and weight of each flower and leaf.

Silk leaves

Silk leaves will fill in the gaps in the traditional mass arrangement when foliage is not easy to come by. If a selection of silk leaves appeals to you choose plain ones rather than variegated, for the variegated ivies, the somewhat brashly-coloured begonias and other brightly-edged and veined silk leaves look very artificial and detract from the flowers. The base leaves in the simple design in colour plate 3 melt into the

PRESERVING PLANT MATERIAL

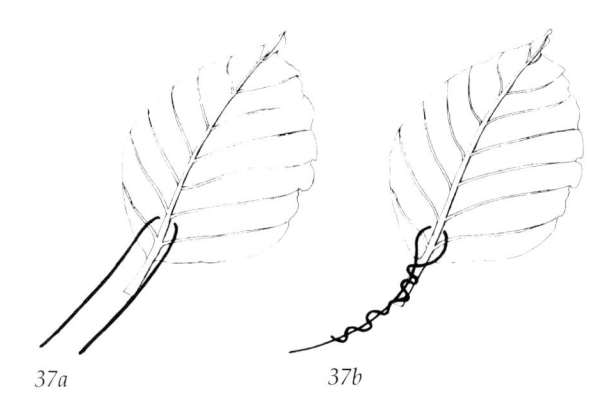

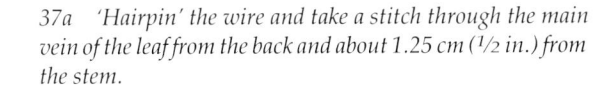

37a

37b

37c

37a   'Hairpin' the wire and take a stitch through the main vein of the leaf from the back and about 1.25 cm (½ in.) from the stem.

37b   Wind one leg of the 'hairpin' round both the other leg of wire and the leaf stem.

37c   Finish by taping the new wire stem.

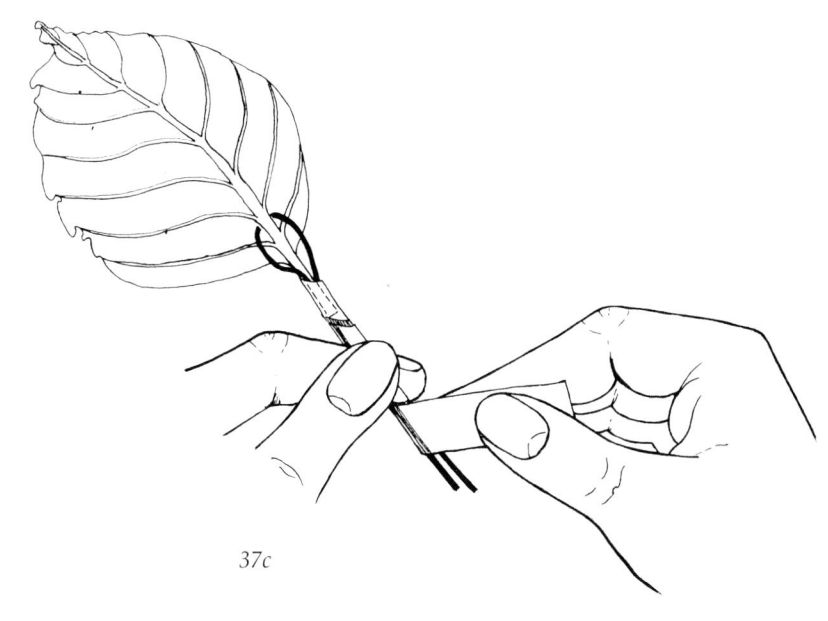

38a and b   Give a silk poppy a strong wire stem to replace the very stiff plastic one. The method is similar to that used in fig. 37.

38c   Finish by taping.

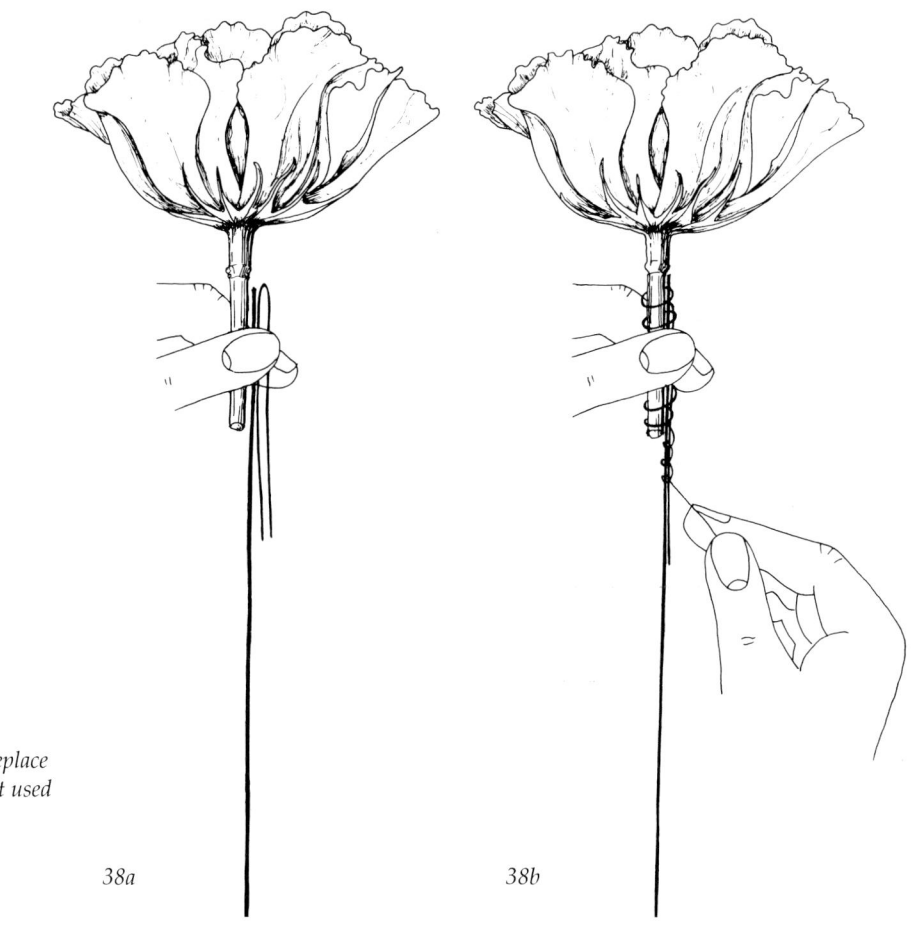

38a

38b

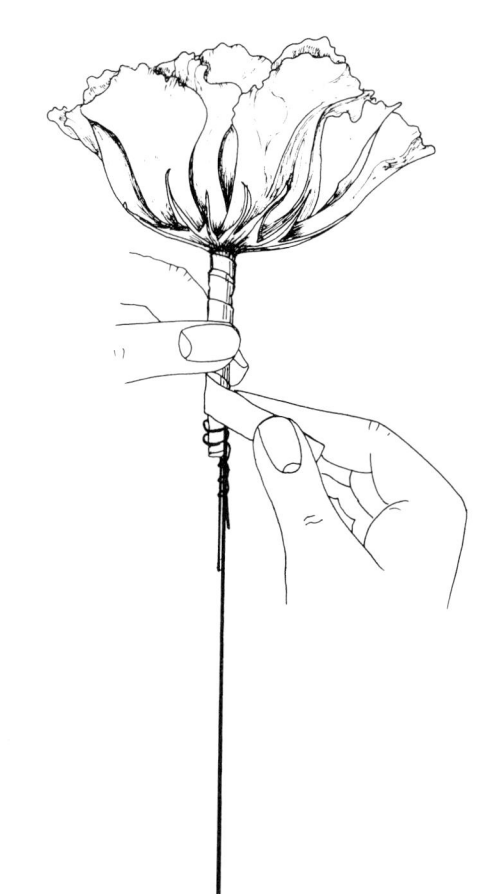

arrangement without holding the eye. Had they been strongly variegated they would have assumed too great an importance. I frequently use similar leaves to those in the picture and I think they are an excellent buy. They were inspired by the plant *Philodendron scandens*, and their shape and size is correct as the leaves measure 8 – 14 cm (3 – 5½ in.) long. They were taken off a stem and wired separately.

Stems for silk flowers

To give silk flowers new and better stems cut off the original plastic ones about 3.75 cm (1½ in.) from the flower head. Then overlap a wire of suitable calibre with the piece of remaining stem so that the new stem wire lies parallel with the shortened flower stem. Next bend in half a thin wire of approximately 15 cm (6 in.) in length – this is called 'hairpinning' – and lay one side of the hairpin alongside the remaining plastic stem and the new stem wire, putting the bend of the hairpin just under the flower head. Twist the free side of the hairpin around the three parallel pieces, making a firm bond. Cover and strengthen the join with tape. This is the classic method of lengthening a stem whether the material is artificial, glycerined or dried. The essential thing is that you have a piece of the original stem attached to the flower or foliage. All wire stems must be taped for not only does this make a neat finish but prevents the wire rusting if it should be put into water or wet Oasis. A delicate leaf or flower can only take a fine wire, but may have a second and stronger one added by hairpinning if necessary.

8
Aids to successful arranging

MECHANICS

Mechanics, in the flower-arranging world, is the collective noun used for the various stem-holding appliances and the different ways and means of putting them into use. Trying to arrange flowers without mechanics is practically impossible. If the top of the container or vase is large they just flop to the sides, and if small, only a few can be put into the opening. In many ways the smaller opening is preferable because the stems will be jammed together and so hold each other in position, enabling the arranger to vary at least the height of each bloom. The success and enjoyment of flower arranging depends completely on correct and reliable mechanics, so I hope the explanations and diagrams in this chapter will be useful.

For those starting from scratch there are essentials to buy that cannot be improvised.

Pinholders

A pinholder or two is absolutely necessary and the tins to put them in must be of the correct height. The Japanese are the creators of the pinholder, which is known to them as the 'Kensan' or 'Sword Mountain'. The proper ones are made with a heavy lead base studded with brass pins set close together. The flower stems and branches are impaled on these pins. Never buy a cheap or a plastic pinholder, or one that is made up of different shapes and can be taken to pieces – they are no good. When in use the brass pins must be covered with water, so the pinholder needs a tin or some sort of container just deep enough to submerge the pins, but shallow enough not to restrict sideways-flowing placements. Paint the tins a matt green, brown or black inside and out so that they will not rust. It must be accepted that very fine-stemmed flowers are not ideal subjects for arranging in a pinholder; flowers placed in these mechanics must have reasonably strong and sizeable stems.

I would suggest the initial purchase of either a 6 cm (2½ in.) or 7.5 cm (3 in.) pinholder and a smaller one that will fit into a yoghurt carton, 4 cm (1½ in.).

39 *When in use the brass pins must be covered with water, so the pinholder needs a tin or some sort of container just deep enough to submerge the pins but shallow enough not to restrict the sideways flow of the plant material.*

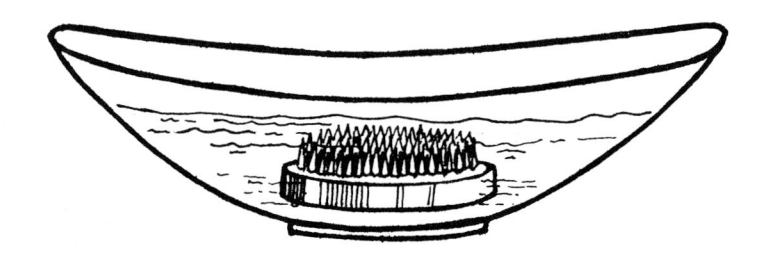

AIDS TO SUCCESSFUL ARRANGING

The well pinholder
The well pinholder is pinholder and container in one. It is a heavy and stable mechanic and a good acquisition, but is less adaptable than the ordinary pinholder. Beware the well pinholder with high steep sides. Buy one with shallow sloping sides. Both well pinholders and ordinary ones will last many years if they are carefully looked after.
If the pins get bent they can easily be straightened.

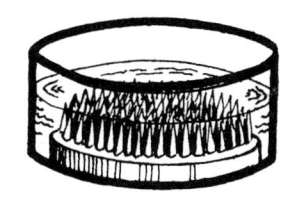

40 A well pinholder (seen here in cross-section) is a pinholder and a container in one.

41 Beware the well pinholder with high steep sides. It prevents the sideways flow of the plant material.

AIDS TO SUCCESSFUL ARRANGING

Wire netting

Plastic-coated wire netting is greatly improved; it used to be very heavy and clumsy. I still prefer plain wire netting from a hardware store, and I recommend 2.5 cm (1 in.) mesh as it is very strong. A small piece wedged into the mouth of a glass container will hold any weight of stems and will not be seen. I am sure that glass containers went out of fashion because it was difficult to find the right mechanics. A pinholder in the bottom of a glass vase looks terrible and Oasis destroys the transparent beauty of glass, preventing you from seeing the stems covered with bubbles. For an opaque bowl a generous amount of crumpled wire netting secured on top of a pinholder gives excellent support for a mass arrangement. The fine, thin stems can be arranged this way too. Fig. 43 shows how valuable the wire netting is when a candlecup is fixed to a bottle.

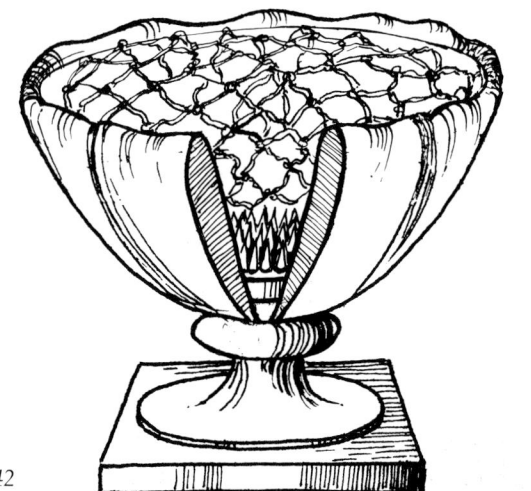

42   *When a bowl is opaque a generous amount of crumpled wire netting on top of a pinholder gives excellent support for a mass arrangement.*

Oasis

There are many brands of floral foam, but possibly the best known is Oasis. These foams are manufactured for both living and preserved plant material, and, of course, both kinds can be used to arrange artificial flowers too. The green blocks, associated with fresh foliage and flowers, must be soaked before being used. The wet Oasis should be moistened every day when in use, and if it is stored away wet it must be enclosed in a plastic bag for it must not be allowed to dry out once it has been soaked or it will not absorb water properly again. Once it is full of holes, throw it away.

Oasis sec
Oasis sec is generally brown, of very gritty texture and made especially for use with dried and glycerined plant material, or artificial flowers. There are now on the market green, brown and white polystyrene balls, rings, hearts, cones and various other shapes. These are *NOT* for use with fresh material and would disintegrate if they were soaked in water. You can recognize Oasis sec by its colour and its shiny, smooth texture.

Oasis containers
There are plastic containers manufactured to take all shapes and sizes of Oasis. A beginner can buy an Oasis 'saucer' for a few

pence and a block of foam to fit it; remember that Oasis takes more plant material than a pinholder and is primarily for the mass arrangement.

CONTAINERS

Cherub containers

Very often it is the gracefulness of a raised arrangement that attracts someone and makes them want to learn how to do it themselves. Be selective when choosing one of the 'cherub'-type containers of which there are now so many, some of good design, but many bad or indifferent. Avoid anything too small that will appear dwarfed by quite a normal-sized arrangement. Also make sure the base of the container is large enough to balance the whole when it has flowers in it. Most important of all is to see that the cup will hold a large enough piece of Oasis – some are hopelessly small. You will get what you pay for as with most other things. The cheaper cherub containers are often a horrible uniform yellowish colour, though this can be toned down with the use of brown or black boot polish, matt paint – two colours mixed – or a burst or two of car spray. Whilst you are keeping your eye open for a raised container that you really like, make do with a bottle or candlestick instead, with the help of a candlecup.

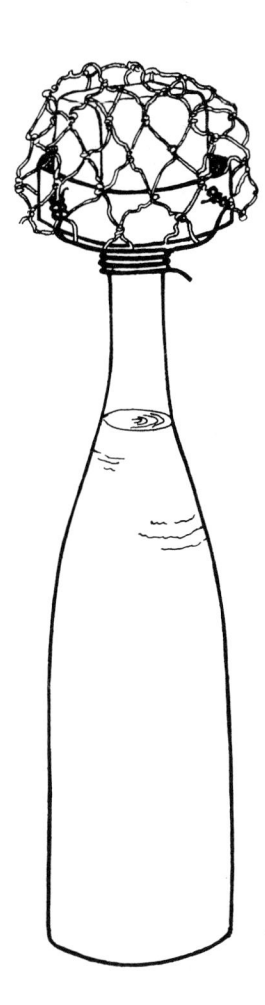

Candlecups

Candlecups are cheap to buy but when they have been correctly fixed onto a candlestick or a bottle they make a raised container that looks very elegant. A green wine bottle is especially attractive for flowers. Take your chosen wine bottle with you when purchasing a candlecup, for bottle openings are not all the same size. To be sure that the candlecup stays firmly in position take extra care in preparing the mechanics.

(1) Fill the bottle with water for ballast, and encircle the neck of the bottle with a piece of stout wire just under the bottle's lip.

(2) Put the candlecup into the top of the bottle and a cube of soaked Oasis into the candlecup. A cube leaves room for watering the foam. The foam should never fill the cup but must always be taller than the cup's rim to allow for a downward flow of plant material.

(3) Cut a piece of 2.5 cm (1 in.) mesh wire netting just large enough to cap the foam and fasten it to the thick wire band on top of the bottle with thin wire. The candlecup will be fastened to the bottle in such a manner that it cannot possibly slip.

43   *A candlecup firmly fixed to a wine bottle filled with water. A cube of Oasis leaves space for watering. The Oasis should never fill the cup but must always be taller than the cup's rim to allow for the downward flow of the plant material.*

Uniting a candlecup to a candlestick can be done in like manner, and in both cases Oasis tape may be substituted for the thick wire, though the result is not quite as reliable.

Jugs and mugs

Every household has an assortment of jugs, mugs and bowls which can be tried out as containers, using a pinholder and/or wire netting for mechanics. Most people also have a selection of empty jars and a tall milk bottle, which can be disguised with a 'pop-over' cover made from strong card or mount board (six sheet) and covered with textured cloth or adhesive covering (see end of chapter). Another good pop-over cover may be made from a plain bamboo or cane place mat. It is also easy to make modern containers out of empty tins weighted with sand and glued together (see fig. 46); these can also be covered with fabric material, Polyfilla or modelling clay. The two latter substances can be textured before they dry and finally painted or sprayed. Model shops have small tins of matt and gloss paint; Humbrol and Airfix neutral shades are especially good.

44 *Pop-over covers for empty jam jars . . .*

AIDS TO SUCCESSFUL ARRANGING

45   . . . and tall milk bottles.

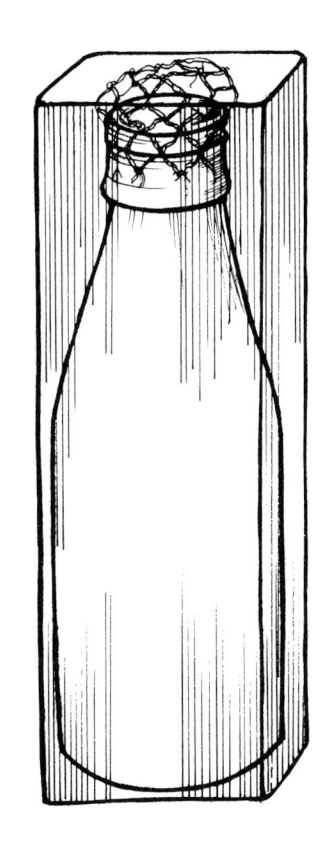

46a, b and c   It is not difficult to make one or two modern containers.

Baskets

Baskets make splendid containers and always seem to look right with flowers. There are so many basket shops around that it is easy to find shapes that appeal. The mechanics for them are simple – a saucer holding Oasis or a pinholder in a tin – but I always add the cap of wire netting, which I then fasten with thin wire from the edge of the wire netting in about three places through the mesh of the basket, securing it at the bottom underneath. Avoid deep baskets, which demand awkwardly high mechanics. Any basket can be painted, and white ones look delicate for small dried arrangements.

OTHER EQUIPMENT

The base

Not every flower arrangement is improved by a base, but one is essential when two placements (two containers holding plant material but making only one complete design) are used, or an accessory is added. (See colour plates 1, 3 and 11.) The base unites the component parts but it also enhances the arrangement just as a picture is enhanced by its frame. Bases can be rush mats, cork mats, or slices of wood, and be painted, sanded or stained.

47   *A base is essential with two placements or when an accessory is added. It unites all the components.*

Oasis tape

This is a green adhesive tape made in different widths (see illustration opposite) for fastening the foam to the container. It is extremely useful, although it does not give the Oasis any extra support for the heavy stems as wire netting does.

Oasis fix

This is a sticky green substance rather like chewing gum that is sold in rolls or in short lengths protected by brown paper. Three very small pieces placed equidistant under a pinholder or Oasis holder will bond to the container as long as both holders and containers are *BONE DRY*. In order to remove the holders, *TWIST* them.

The Oasis holder

An Oasis holder looks like a pinholder but it has only a few long pins set into a heavy lead base. The purpose of the Oasis holder is two-fold: to provide base weight and to hold the Oasis firmly on the pins so that it cannot shift about in the container. It is best to remove a matching-sized circle of Oasis to allow the Oasis holder to lie level with the bottom of the block, so that both Oasis and holder are flush with the container.

AIDS TO SUCCESSFUL ARRANGING

The sprog or frog

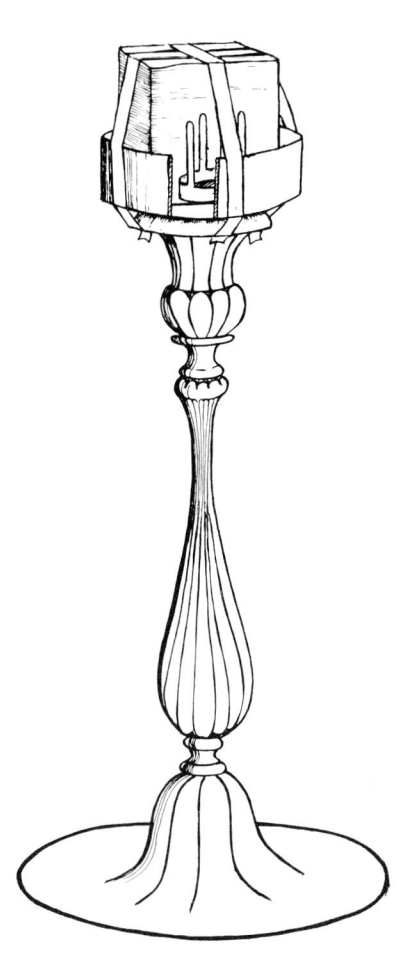

The sprog or frog is a lightweight plastic version of the Oasis holder. It only costs a few pence. It is green and has four pins. Although it provides no base weight for an arrangement, it is excellent in candlecups and the bowls of cherub containers, for it stops any movement of the Oasis (fig. 48).

'Pop-over' covers

These covers have no base and so they are very quickly made. A sheet of mount board such as Daler (six sheet), glue, adhesive covering (e.g. Fablon), a sharp knife and a ruler are all that is required.

For the tall milk bottle cover:
– Cut a length of mount board 32.5 cm long x 22.5 cm high (13 x 9 in.)
– With a Stanley knife or other sharp craft knife score down the divisions
– Bend into a square and glue the open sides
– Cut the adhesive material allowing 1.25 cm (½ in.) overlap all round, top and bottom included
– Cover with adhesive material

For a jam jar follow the same method but cut the mount board 32 cm long x 13 cm high (13 x 5½ in.).

48 Oasis tape holds the foam, which is, in turn, impaled on a sprog in the candlecup.

DISPLAY AND LIGHTING

Every home has places where flowers show to their greatest advantage. Such areas may be natural or deliberately created, but usually once established, these positions tend not to be varied. The top of a bookcase against a plain matt painted wall makes a good display point; flowers there could be at eye level and are in no danger of being knocked over. Wall vases or arrangements on small wall shelves (see colour plate 10) are also safely out of reach of children; neither do they take up valuable surface space in limited living quarters. The coffee table design, made to look down on, is not practical for every day in a living room used by a growing family with its many interests and pursuits. Neither is the dining-room table decoration possible when the same table is needed for homework and a hundred and one other occupations. Arrangements in such places must be for special events, but for everyday use find a surface where a container can stand safely but where it will make a point of interest in the home.

It is inevitable that the height, background, size and lighting of the chosen position will dictate the style, scale and colour of the flower arrangement. The amount of available light falling on the flowers has to be reckoned with, for blue, purple and maroon will disappear in a poor light. Vibrant advancing colours of yellow, orange, lime green, clear bright red, white and tints containing white are best in a darkish room, and the receding hues can be enjoyed in the well-lit conditions of mid-summer.

Artificial light

Dramatic effects can be created with artificial lighting, but remember that colours are changed, not only by their surroundings, but by various types of light. Daylight is the truest, and gives to all colours their real value. Fluorescent lighting turns reds and oranges brownish, whilst giving blues their true hues. The opposite happens with the ordinary tungsten bulb: the reds remain clear but the blues tend to vanish.

A spotlight will certainly emphasize an arrangement but will prove too hot and result in the flowers wilting before their time. Any light bulb placed close to plant material will cause this to happen. Light behind an arrangement silhouettes its outline and the shapes of the flowers. Light falling on a design from the front will cast some shadows on the background – the brighter the light the heavier the shadows, and in order to eliminate these some light has to be directed behind the flowers. However, shadows make for interest, and a low front light will throw fascinating shadows on the ceiling. Do experiment with colours, containers and lighting effects, for this is all a part of the pleasure to be had from arranging natural plant material.

Appendix

WIRE GAUGE MEASURES

Wire thickness

Wire thickness (mm)	Equivalent gauge No (swg)
1.25	18
1.00	19
0.90	20
0.71	22
0.56	24
0.46	26
0.38	28
0.32	30
0.28	32
0.24	34
0.20	36

Wire lengths

Metric (mm)	Imperial (in.)
90	3½
100	4
130	5
200	8
230	9
260	10
310	12
360	14
380	15
460	18

Index

Air lock 12, 34
Anemone 43, 46
Annual 24–5, 29, 32–3

Base 15, 19, 89, 118
Baskets 22, 81, 88, 90, 118
Biennial 29
Bleaching 100–101
Blossom 19–20, 22
Broom handle 54–6
Bulbs 36, 77–80

Cacti 67
Campanula 24–5, 29–30
Candlecup 112, 115–16
Car body spray 69
Carnation 31, 34, 43, 51, 103
Cellulose filler *see* Polyfilla
Chionodoxa 21
Christmas 11, 21, 43, 50, 100
Christmas decorations 50–53, 59
Christmas rose 48, 51–2, 59
Chrysanthemum 11, 36, 38, 40, 44, 71
Cling film 53, 56, 58, 61
Collage 97–8
Concrete 54, 56
Conditioning 18–19, 34–5, 46–7, 50
Cone 40, 59–60, 86
Container 15, 19–20, 32, 45, 47–8, 68–72, 77–9, 88, 90, 111–18
Cornflower 28

Covering a pot 53–4
Cow parsley 100

Daffodil 11, 14–16, 19
Dahlia 24, 37–8, 43, 71
Defoliation 34–5
Delphinium 24–5, 29–30, 33
Dianthus 28
Door ring *see* Wreath
Dowelling rod 54, 56
Drying flowers 30–31, 88, 91, 97, 101–3, 107

Fatshedera 23
Foam
  dry 52–3, 60, 113
  water retaining 16, 47, 52–3
  see also Oasis
Forsythia 19
Foxglove 15
Freesia 31, 43, 47–8
Fruit 36, 40, 59, 82–7

Gaillardia 24
Garland 39, 46, 52, 62–3
Gerbera 31, 43
Gladioli 16, 24, 31–2, 42, 71
Glass 12, 14, 45, 112
Glycerining foliage 22–3, 91, 93–5, 107
Grape hyacinth 21

INDEX

Hair lacquer 31
Half-hardy annual 29
Hawthorn 20
Heather 15
Helenium 24
Helianthus 24
Helichrysum 36, 97, 99, 103
Helipterum 99
Hellebore 48, 50
Holly 51
Hyacinth 36

Iris 15
Ivy 15, 45, 51

Kingcup 15

Landscape style 20, 45
Larkspur 30, 34
Lighting 112–13
Lilac 19
Lily 34, 40, 71
Limonium see Statice
Lupin 24

Mechanics 84–5, 87–8, 109, 120–21
Metallic spray 14, 55, 57, 63, 86
Mistletoe 51
Mounting board 116

Nerine 40–41

Oasis (see also Foam) 12, 50–56, 58–60, 85, 108, 112–14, 118

Peony 24
Perennial 24, 29
Pinholder 15–16, 32, 52, 66, 109–11, 114, 118
Pinks 24
Polyanthus 21–2
Polyfilla (cellulose filler) 55, 57, 116
Polystyrene 53, 55, 113
Pop-over cover 32, 48, 116, 121
Pot-et-fleur 21, 32, 40, 43, 66–81
  suitable plants for 76–7
Pressed picture 37, 91
Pressing flowers 91, 93
Primrose 20–21
Prunus triloba 19
Pussy willow 22
Pyrethrum 24

Reedmace 15
Ribbon 51, 59–60, 62
Rose 27, 31, 35, 43
Rudbeckia 24–5

Scabious 24
Schizostylis 42
Scilla 21
Selecting plant material 11–12, 18, 26, 33

INDEX

Silk flowers 10, 15, 20, 45, 50, 62, 81, 84, 86, 91, 103–7
Snowdrop 44
Statice 99
Stem-taping 51, 63–5, 86, 89, 99, 106–7
Stem-wiring 51, 53, 63–5, 86, 89, 99, 102–7
Succulent 67, 73
Swag 39, 52

Tulip 16–18
Topiary tree 40, 52–3

Umbelliferae family 100

Vegetables 81
Violet 21

Wire netting 14, 32, 47, 53, 59, 90, 112
Wood 14–15, 19
Wreath 52, 57–9, 62